SIXTEEN REVELATIONS OF DIVINE LOVE,

MADE TO A DEVOUT SERVANT OF OUR LORD, CALLED

Mother Juliana,

AN ANCHORETE OF NORWICH:

Who lived in the days of King Edward the Third

XVI REVELATIONS OF DIVINE LOVE,

Shewed to a Devout Servant of our Lord, called

MOTHER JULIANA,

AN ANCHORETE OF NORWICH:

Who lived in the days of King Edward the Third

GYAN

ISBN : 978-81-212-9026-5 (HB)

First Published, 1902

Indian Reprint in 2017

Published by

Gyan Publishing House
5, Ansari Road
Daryaganj, New Delhi-110002
Phone: 9811692060
E-mail: books@gyanbooks.com

Printed at: G. Print Process, Delhi.

PREFACE

TO THE PRESENT EDITION.

The following singular work contains so much interesting matter, that I am inclined to hope the present reprint will not be unfavourably received; more especially, as I have reason to know that this book, in common with the rest of Cressy's publications, has become scarce; either because few were originally printed, or copies may lie buried in the libraries of old popish families, or they may have perished in the lapse of time. In the catalogue of his publications in Dodd's Church History, the title of the volume is as follows: "Sixteen Revelations of Divine Love shewed to a devout servant of our Lord called Mother Juliana, a devout anchorete of Norwich; who lived in the days of King Edward 3rd; revived from an ancient copy, and dedicated to Mary

Lady Blount, of Sodington, widow of Sir George Blount. 8vo. 1670."

Hugh Paulin Cressey, or Cressy, (the original editor) descended from an ancient and genteel family, was born at Wakefield in Yorkshire. In 1619, when fourteen years old, he was sent to the University of Oxford. In 1625 he was elected probationer of Merton College, and in the year after was made true and perpetual Fellow. After he had taken the degree of Master of Arts, and had entered into holy orders, he became Chaplain to Thom. Lord Wentworth, while he was President of the North, and afterwards when he was Earl of Strafford. In 1638, he went into Ireland, in the quality of Chaplain, as is supposed, with Lucius Lord Falkland. In the latter end of 1642 he became Canon of Windsor, but was never installed in that dignity, and much about the same time had the Deanery of Laighlen in Ireland conferred upon him. In 1646 he made a public recantation at Rome, before the Inquisition, of the Protestant faith. He afterwards went to Paris, and there published, Exomologesis: or, a faithful narration of the occasions and motives that induced him to change his religion: Paris, 1647 and 53, in octavo, a copy of which he sent to his dear friend Dr. Henry Hammond. When at Paris, Henrietta Maria, Queen of England, rendered him services. Ultimately, upon invitation he went to Douay, and took upon him the habit of the Benedictine order in the college of the English monks at that place: changing his name to Serenus De Cressey. After having lived according to their discipline for seven years or more, he became one of the mission in England. At length upon the King's marriage with Katherine the Infanta of Portugal, he became one of her servants, and mostly lived at Somerset House. He was reputed the Coryphæus of the Roman party: but while at Oxford was accounted a quick and accurate disputant, a man of a good nature, manners, and natural parts, and when in orders, no inconsiderable preacher. He is also said to have been peculiarly temperate in controversy. After he returned to England, his former acquaintance found great alterations in him as to parts and vivacity, and he seemed to some to be possessed with strange notions, and to others, a reserved person, and little better than a melancholic. Which mutation arose, not perhaps known to him, upon his solely giving himself up to religion, the refinedness of his soul, and the avoiding of all matters relating to human and prophane learning, as vanities. He died at East Greensted in Sussex in 1674, and was, it is believed, buried in the Church of that place.

The above account is taken from Wood's Athenæ Oxon. where a catalogue of his works may be found. See also, Dodd's Church History—Chalmers' Biographical Dictionary, voce Cressey—and the Biographia Britannica, 2nd edition.

The spiritually-minded reader will meet with some few statements in the course of the following pages, in which he will not be able to acquiesce; but in the main he will meet with much amply to repay a careful perusal.

The Authoress, a pious recluse of the name of Juliana, was contemporary with Wiclif; it does not however appear that she had any connection with his party; the work before us bears independent witness to the truth, and is peculiarly interesting as a devotional treatise of the fourteenth century.

I do not venture to pass any judgment as to how

far these Revelations may be imputed to a fevered imagination: to whatever cause we attribute them, the overruling hand of God for good must be recognized.

Viewed as a religious composition, the present volume comprises much of deep Christian doctrine and experience: affording us a fresh testimony to the fact that the Spirit of God is able to lead His people into all saving truth under the most disadvantageous circumstances: it reminds us that He is not confined to means: it gives us additional cause to rest assured that in all ages God has had a seed to serve Him; and confirms our belief that even during the worst corruptions of the Romish Church there was a generation within its pale, who, though unknown to history and labouring under many imperfections, yet held the Head Christ; and formed a part of that vital bond which connected the Apostolic Church with the revival of primitive Christianity at the times of the Reformation. It is very interesting to trace the strugglings of the writer's mind against preconceived and erroneous opinions.

Considerable attention will be found requisite in the perusal of the following pages. The matter is peculiar;

the style quaint; and the language obscure. I have compiled a glossary of obsolete words and phrases, in which I have been aided by Tyrwhitt's Glossary to Chaucer—Nares' Archaiological Glossary—and Bosworth's Anglo-Saxon Dictionary.

It is sometimes difficult to discover whether words enclosed within parentheses were in the original manuscript or not: sometimes they appear like glosses of the transcriber. The work is printed verbatim et literatim from the edition of 1670, except in one or two instances where a typographical error was obvious.

G. H. PARKER.

GROBY,

JANUARY 11, 1843.

TO HIS MOST HONOURED LADY, THE LADY MARY BLOUNT, OF SODINGTON.

MADAM,

THE just and grateful resentment which I have of the unmerited kindness, and friendship of your late most worthy and noble husband Sir George Blount, of your Ladiship, and your whole family, obliged me, impatiently to desire an occasion, to make a public acknowledgement thereof. Permit me therefore here, to offer to your Ladyship this small present, in which notwithstanding, I can challenge no interest or right, but only the care of publishing it. The author of it, is a person of your own sex, who lived about three hundred years since, intended it for you, and for such readers as your self, who will not be induced to the perusing of it by curiosity, or a desire to learn strange things, which afterward they will at best vainly admire, or perhaps out of incredulity contemn.

But your Ladiship will, I assure myself, afford her a place in your closet, where at your devout retirements, you will enjoy her saint-like conversation, attending to her, whilst with humility and joy, she recounts to you the wonders of our Lords love to her, and of his grace in her. And being thus employed, I make no doubt but you will be sensible of many beams of her lights, and much warmth of her charity, by reflection darted into your own soul. Now that such may be the effects of this book, is the desire of

(Madam)

Your Ladyships most humble,

and most obliged Servant

in our Lord,

H. CRESSY.

TO THE READER.

DEVOUT READER,

WHATSOEVER benefit thou mayest reap by this book, thou art obliged for it to a more venerable Abbot* of our nation, by whose order and liberality it is now published, and by consequence sufficiently approved.

I conceived it would have been a prejudice to the agreeable simplicity of the stile, to have changed the dress of it into our modern language, as some advised. Yet certain more out of fashion, words or phrases, I thought meet to explain in the margine.†

I was desirous to have told thee somewhat of the happy virgin, the compiler of these Revelations: but after all the search I could make, I could not discover any thing touching her, more than what she occasionally sprinkles in the book

* The V. R. F. Jo. Guscoyn Lo. Abbot of Lambspring.

† In this edition the explanations have been taken out of the margin, and put together in the form of a Glossary at the end of the volume.

it self. The postscript acquaints us with her name, Juliana: as likewise her profession, which was of the strictest sort of solitary livers; being inclosed all her life (alone) within four walls: whereby, though all mortals were excluded from her dwelling, yet saints and angels, and the Supream King of both, could, and did find admittance. Moreover, in the same postscript we find, that the place in a high manner dignified by her abode, and by the access of her heavenly guest, was the City of Norwich. The time when she lived, and particularly, when these celestial Revelations were afforded her, she her self in the beginning of the book informes us, was in the year of grace MCCCLXXIII. that is, about three years before the death of the famous conquerour, King Edward the Third: at which time she her self was about thirty years of age. And to conclude, in the last chapter of the book she signifies, that more than fifteen years after these Revelations had been shewed her, how for resolution of a certain doubt of hers touching the meaning of one of them, our Lord himself was pleased to answer her internally in ghostly understanding.

As for the manner of these Revelations, it was the same of which we read innumerable examples, both among ancient and modern saints. The objects of some of them were represented to the imagination, and perhaps also to the outward sight; sometimes they were represented in sleep, but most frequently when she was awake. But those which were more pure, intime and withall more certain, were wrought by a divine illapse into the spiritual part of the soul, the mind and understanding, which the devil cannot counterfeit, nor the patient comprehend, though withal it excluded all doubt or suspicion of illusion.

But the principal thing which I desire to recommend to the reader's consideration, is the preceding occasion, and subsequent effects of these divine favours bestowed by Almighty God on his humble devout handmaid.

She was far from expecting, or desiring such unusual supernatural gifts. Matters stood thus with her: she thought her self too much unmortified in her affection to creatures, and too unsensible of our Lords love to her. Therefore to cure the former, she requested a sickness in extremity, even to death, in her own and others conceit; a sickness full of bitter pain and anguish, depriving her of all outward refreshments, and of all inward comforts also, which might affect the sensual portion of the soul. And for a remedy to the latter, she begged of our Lord, that he would imprint in her soul, by what way he thought best, a deep and vigorous conception, and resentment of those most violent torments, which he in his infinite love suffered for her on the cross, to the end she might be even forced to return to him a suitable affection.

Yet in making these requests, she expressed a perfect resignation (as to the manner) to his heavenly will. The only graces that she did, and might, and so may we, desire absolutely, without any condition, were a true spiritual hatred and contempt of her self, and of all worldly, or sensual contentments; a perfect sorrow and compunction for sins past; and a cordial love, and reverential fear of Almighty God. These were the gifts she desired: and as for the means of procuring these graces, she proposed the best to her seeming: yet so, as being assured that God knew what was best for her, she left them to his Divine pleasure.

It was, no doubt, by Divine inspiration, that she at first made such petitions, both for the substance and manner, and therefore God granted them as she desired; yea, in a manner more extraordinary than she durst pretend to, as the reader may observe. And how wonderful the effects of them were, the whole contexture of her discourses upon each Revelation will excellently demonstrate.

And now, since she her self professes, that the lights and

torches which God was pleased to give her, were intended not for her self alone, but for the universality of God's true servants, for whose benefit also she wrote them, the devout reader will, I hope, think himself obliged not to content himself with a fruitless admiring, but will, after her example, aspire to alike affectuous, operative contemplation of the meer nothingness of creatures, of the inconceivable ugliness of sin, of the infinite tenderness and indefectibility of God's love to his elect, and of the omnipotency of Divine grace working in them; to which grace alone all good in us is to be ascribed.

XVI. REVELATIONS

OF

LOVE.

Here beginneth the First Chapter.

THIS is a Revelation of Love, that Jesu Christ our endless blisse made in xvi. shewings: of which,

The *first* is of his precious crowning of thornes, and therein was conteined and specified the blessed Trinity, with the incarnation and the uniting between God and mans soul, with manie faire shewings and teachings of endeless wisdom and love: in which all the shewings that follow be grounded and joyned.

The *second*, is of the discolouring of his faire face, in tokening of his dear worthie passion.

The *third* is, that our Lord God Almighty, all wisdom and all love, right also verilie as he hath made all thinges that are right, also verilie he doth and worketh all things that are done.

The *fourth* is, scourging of his tender bodie with plenteous shedding of his precious blood.

The *fifth* is, that the fiend is overcome by the precious passion of Christ.

The *sixth* is, the worshipfull thanking of our Lord God, in which he rewardeth all his blessed servants in heaven.

The *seventh* is, oftentimes feeling of weale and woe. Feeling of weale is gracious touching and lightning, with true sikernes of endeles joy: the feeling of woe is of temptation by heavines, and wearines of our fleshlie living with ghostelie understanding, that we be kept also verelie in love, in woe as in weal, by the goodnes of God.

The *eighth* is, the last paines of Christ and his cruell dying.

The *ninth* is, of the liking which is in the blessed Trinity of the hard passion of Christ after his rufull and sorrowful dying: in which joy and liking he will that we be in solace and mirth with him, till that we come to the glorie in heaven.

The *tenth* is, our Lord Jesu Christ by love his blessed heart even cloven in two.

The *eleventh* is, an high ghostlie shewing of his deare worthie Mother.

The *twelfth* is, that our Lord God is all soveraign being.

The *thirteenth* is, that our Lord God will that we have great regard to all the deedes which he hath done in the great nobletie of all things making, and of the excellency of mans making, the which is above all his works; and of the precious *amends* that he hath made for mans sin, turning all our blame into endeles worship. Than meaneth he thus, '*Beholde and see, for by the same might, wisdome and goodness that I have done all this, by the same might, wisdome and goodness I shall make well all that is not well, and thou shalt see it.*' And in this he will that we keep us in the faith and truth of Holie Church, not willing to wit his privities, not but as it longeth to us in this life.

The *fourteenth* is, that our Lord God is the ground of our beseekinge. Herein was seen *two* fair properties: that *one* is rightful praier: that *other* is verie trust, which he will both be one like large, and thus our praier liketh him, and he of his goodness fulfilleth it.

The *fifteenth* is, that we should soudeinlie be taken from all our paine, and from all our woe, and of his goodnes we shall come up above, where we shall have our Lord Jesu to our meed, and for to be fulfilled with joy and blisse in heaven.

The *sixteenth* is, that the blessed Trinitie, our maker in Christ Jesu our Saviour, endleslie dwelleth in our soule, worshipfullie rewarding and commanding all things, us mightilie and wiselie saving and keeping for love, and we shall not be over-come of our enemy.

The Second Chapter.

THIS Revelation was made to a simple creature unlettered, living in deadlie flesh, the year of our Lord, a thousand three hundreth lxxiij, the xiiij*th* daie of Maie: which creature desired before *three* gifts by the grace of God.

The *first*, was mind of the passion.

The *second*, was bodilie sickness.

The *third*, was to have of Gods gift three woundes. For the first, me thought I had some deale feeling in the passion of Christ, but yet I desired to have more by the grace of God. Me thought I would have been that time with Magdalen, and with other that were Christs lovers, that I might have seen bodilie the passion that our Lord suffered for me, that I might have suffered with him as others did that loved him; and therefore I desired a bodilie sight, wherein I might have more knowledge of the bodilie paines of our Saviour, and of the compassion of our Lady, and of all his true lovers that were living that time, and saw his paines: for I would have bene one of them, and have suffered with them. Other sight nor shewing of God desired I never none, till when the soule were departed from the body, for I believed to be saved by the mercy of God. This was my meaning; for I would after because of that shewing have the more true mind in the passion of

Christ. For the *second* came to my mind with contrition freelie, without anie seeking, a wilfull desire to have of Gods gift, a bodilie sicknes. I would that that sicknes were so hard as to the death, that I might in that sicknes have undertaken all the Rights of Holie Church, my self weening that I should have died, and that all creatures might suppose the same that saw me: for I would have no manner of comfort of fleshly, ne earthly life in that sicknes. I desired to have all manner of paines, bodilie and ghostlie, that I should have if I should have died: all the dreads and temptations of fiends, and all manner of other paines, saving the out-passing of the soule. And this meant I, for I would be purged by the mercy of God, and after live more to the worship of God because of that sicknes. For I hoped that it might have bene to my reward when I should have died, for I desired to have bene soone with my God and Maker.

These two desires of the passion, and of the sicknes that I desired of him, was with a condition: for me thought this was not the common use of praier. Therefore I said, 'Lord thou knowest what I would, and if that it be thy will that I might have it; and if it be not thy will, good Lord, be not displeased, for I will not but as thou wilt.'

This sicknes I desired in my youth, that I might have it when I were thirtie years old.

For the third, by the grace of God and teaching of

Holie Church, I conceived a mightie desire to receive *three* wounds in my life, that is to say, the wound of verie *contrition*, the wound of kind *compassion*, and the wound of *willful longing* to God.

Right as I asked the other twaine with a condition, so asked I this third mightilie without any condition. These twaine desires before said, passed from my mind, and the third dwelled continuallie.

The Third Chapter.

AND when I was thirtie yeares old and a halfe, God sent me a bodilie sicknes, in which I lay three daies and three nights, and on the fourth night, I tooke all my Rights of Holie Church, and went not to have liven till daie. And after this I laie two daies and two nights, and on the third night I weened oftentimes to have passed, and so weened they that were with me, and yet in this I felt a great loathness to die, but for nothing that was in earth that me liketh to live for, ne for no paine that I was afraid of, for I trusted in God of his mercy: but it was, for I would have lived to have loved God better, and a longer time; that I might by the grace of that living have the more knowing and loving of God in the blisse of heaven. For methought all that time that I had lived here, so litle and so short in regarde of that endles blisse, I thought, 'Good Lord, may my living be no longer to thy worshippe?'

And I understood in my reason, and by the feeling of my paines that I should die: and I assented fullie with all the will of myne heart to be at Gods will.

Thus I endured till daie, and by then was my bodie dead from the middes downwarde, as to my feeling.

Then was I holpen to be sett upright, undersett with help, for to have the more freedome of my heart to be at Gods will, and thinking on God while my life lasted.

My Curate was sent for to be at my ending, and before he came I had sett up my eien, and might not speak. He sett the crosse before my face, and said, "I have brought the image of our Saviour, looke thereupon and comfort thee therewith." Me thought I was well, for my eien were sett upright into heaven, where I trusted to come by the mercy of God.

But neverthelesse I assented to sett my eien in the face of the crucifix, if I might, and so I did; for me thought I might longer dure to looke even forth than right up. After this my sight began to faile, it waxed as darke about me in the chamber as if it had bene night, save in the image of the crosse, wherein held a common light, and I wist not how; all that was besides the crosse was uglie and fearefull to me, as it had bene much occupied with fiendes.

After this the over-parte of my bodie began to die, so farre forth that unneath I had any feeling; my most paine was shortnes of breath, and failing of life.

Then went I verilie to have passed, and in this case sodenlie all my paine was taken from me, and I was as whole, and namely in the over-part of my bodie, as ever I was before. I marvailed of this sodaine change: for me thought that it was a privie working of God, and not of kind. And yet by feeling of this ease, I trusted never the more to have lived; ne the feeling of this ease was no full ease unto me: for me thought I had rather have bene delivered of this world, for my heart was wilfullie sett thereto.

Then came sodeinlie to my minde, that I should desire the seconde wound of our Lords gift, and of his grace, that my bodie might be fulfilled with mind and feeling of his blessed passion, as I had before praied. For I would that his paines were my paines with compassion, and afterwards longing to God.

Thus thought me, that I might with his grace have the wounds that I had before desired. But in this I desired never no bodilie sight; ne no manner shewing of God, but compassion, as me thought that a kind soule might have with our Lord Jesu, that for love would become a deadlie man with him. I desired to suffer living in my deadlie bodie, as God would give me grace.

The First Revelation.

The Fourth Chapter.

AND in this, sodeinlie I saw the red blood running down from under the garland, hott and freshly, plenteouslie and livelie, right as it was in the time that the garland of thornes was pressed on his blessed head, right so both God and man the same that suffered for me. I conceaved trulie and mightilie that it was himself that shewed it me without any meane.

And in the same shewing, sodeinlie the Trinitie fulfilled my heart most of joy: and so I understood it shall be in heaven without end to all that shall come there. For the Trinitie is God. God is the Trinitie, the Trinitie is our Maker, the Trinitie is our Keeper, the Trinitie is our everlasting Lover, the Trinitie is our endles joy and our blisse, by our Lord Jesu Christ, and in our Lord Jesu Christ: and this was shewed in the first sight, and in all. For when Jesu appeareth, the blessed Trinity is understood as unto my sight.

And I said, *Benedicite dominus*. This I said for reverence in my meaning with a mightie voice, and full greatelie was I astonished for wonder and marveile that I had, that he that is so reverent and so dreadful will be so homelie with a sinfull creature living in this wretched flesh.

Thus I tooke it for that time that our Lord Jesu of his courteous love would shew me comfort before the time of my temptation: for me thought it might well be, that I should by the sufferance of God, and with his keeping, be tempted of fiends before I should die.

With this sight of his blessed passion, with the Godhead that I sawe in my understanding, I knew well that it was strength enough to me, yea and to all creatures living, that should be saved against all the fiendes of hell, and against all ghostlie enemies.

In this he brought our Lady Saint Mary to my understanding; I sawe her ghostelie in bodilie likenes, a simple maiden and a meeke, young of age, a litle waxen above a child, in the stature as she was when she conceived.

Also God shewed me in part the wisdome and the truth of her soule; wherein I understood the reverence beholding that she beheld her God that is her Maker, marvailing with great reverence that he would be born of her that was a simple creature of his making.

For this was her marvailing, that he that was her Maker would be born of her that was made.

And this wisdome and truth knowing the greatnes of her Maker, and the litlehead of her selfe that is made, made her to saie full meekelie to Gabriel, 'Lo me here Gods hand-maiden.'

In this sight I did understand verilie that she is more than all that God made beneath her in worthines and full-head; for above her is nothing that is made but the blessed manhood of Christ, as to my sight.

The Fifth Chapter.

In this same time that I sawe this sight of the head bleeding, our good Lord shewed a ghostlie sight of his homelie loving: I saw that he is to us all thing that is good and comfortable to our help.

He is our clothing, that for love wrappeth us, and windeth us, halseth us, and all beclosetlı us, hangeth about us for tender love, that he maie never leave us. And so in this sight I saw that he is all thing that is good, as to my understanding.

And in this he shewed a litle thing, the quantitie of a hasel-nutt, lying in the palme of my hand, as me seemed; and it was as round as a ball. I looked theron with the eie of my understanding, and thought, "What may this be?" and it was answered generallie thus.

'*It is all that is made.*' I marvelled how it might last: for me thought it might sodenlie have fallen to naught for litlenes.

And I was answered in my understanding, '*It lasteth,*

and ever shall: for God loveth it. And so hath all thing being by the love of God.'

In this litle thing I sawe three propeties.

The *first* is, that God made it.

The *second* is, that God loveth it.

The *third* is, that God keepeth it.

But, what beheld I therein? verilie the Maker, the Keeper, the Lover. For till I am substanciallie united to him, I maie never have full rest, ne verie blisse; that is to saie, that I be so fastned to him, that there be right nought that is made betweene my God and mee.

This litle thing that is made, me thought it might have fallen to nought for litleness.

Of this needeth us to have knowledge, that us liketh naught all thing that is made, for to love God, and have God that is unmade.

For this is the cause which we be not all in ease of heart and soule: for we seeke here rest in this thing that is so litle, where no rest is in: and we know not our God that is all mightie, all wise, and all good, for he is verie rest.

God will be known, and him liketh that we rest us in him.

For all that is beneath him, sufficeth not us.

And this is the cause why that no soule is in rest till it is naughted of all things that are made: when she is wilfullie naughted for love to have him that is all, then is she able to receave ghostlie rest.

And also our good Lord shewed, that it is full great pleasure to him that a seelie soule come to him naked, plainlie, and homelie. For this is the kind dwelling of the soule by the touching of the Holie Ghost, as by the understanding that I have in this shewing. 'God of thy goodnes give me thy self, for thou art enough to me; and I may aske nothing that is lesse, that may be fullie worship to thee; and if I aske any thing that is lesse, ever me wanteth. But onlie in thee I have all.'

And these wordes of the goodnes of God be full lovesome to the soule, and full nere touching the will of our Lord; for his goodnes fulfilleth all his creatures, and all his blessed works without end.

For he is the endlesse head, and he made us onlie to himselfe: and restored us by his precious passion, and ever keepeth us in his blessed love; and all this is of his goodnes.

The Sixth Chapter.

THIS shewing was given to my understanding, to learne our soule wisely to cleave to the goodnes of God, and in that same time the custome of our praier was brought to my mind, how that we use, for unknowing of love, to make many meanes. Then sawe I verilie that it is more worship to God, and more verie delight that we faithfullie pray to himself of his goodnes, and cleave therto by his grace with true understanding and stedfast beleif, then if we made all the meanes that heart may think.

For if we make all these meanes, it is too litle, and not full worship to God: but in his goodnes is all the whole; and there faileth right nought.

For thus as I shall saie, came to my minde in the same time: we pray to God for his holie flesh, and for his precious blood, his holie passion, his deare worthie death, and worshipfull wounds; for all the blessed kindenes and the endles life that we have of all this, it is of the goodnes of God. And we praie him for his sweet mothers love that bare him; and all the helpe that we have of her it is of his goodnes. And we praie for his holie crosse that he died on; and all the helpe, and all the vertue of that we have of that crosse, it is of his goodnes.

And on the same wise, all the helpe that we have to special saints, and of all the blessed companie of heaven; the deare worthie love, and the holy endles friendship that we have of them, it is of his goodness.

For the meanes that the goodnes of God hath ordeined for to helpe us, be full faire and many.

Of which the chiefe and principall meane is the blessed kinde that he took of the maiden, with all the meanes that went before, and come after, which be longing to our redemption and to our endless salvation.

Wherefore it pleaseth him, that we seeke him, and worship him by meanes; understanding, and knowing that he is the goodnes of all.

For to the goodnes of God is the highest praier, and it cometh down to us to the lowest partie of our neede; it quickneth our soule, and maketh it live, and makes it to waxe in grace and vertue; it is nearest in kind and readiest in grace.

For it is the same grace that the soule seeketh, and ever shall till we know our God verilie that hath us all in himself beclosed.

A man goeth upright, and the soule of his body is sparred as a purse full faire, and when it is time of his necessity, it is opened and sparred againe full honestlie.

And that it is he that doth this, it is shewed there where he saith, '*He cometh downe to us to the lowest part of our need.*' For he hath no despite of that he made, ne hath he no disdaine to serve us at the simplest office that to our bodie longeth in kind, for love of the soule that he made to his own likenes.

For as the bodie is cladd in the cloath, and the flesh in the skinn, and the bones in the flesh, and the heart in the bulke, so are we soule and bodie cladd and enclosed in the goodnes of God: yea, and more homelie, for all they vanish and wast away, the goodnes of God is ever whole and more nere to us without any comparison.

For truelie our Lover desireth that the soule cleave to

him with all the mightes, and that we be evermore cleaving to his goodnes: for of all thing that heart can thinke it pleaseth most God, and soonest speedeth.

For our soule is so preciouslie loved of him that is highest, that it over-passeth the knowing of all creatures:

That is to saie, there is no creature that is made, that may wit how much, and how sweetly, and how tenderlie that our Maker loveth us. And therefore, we may with his grace and his helpe, stand in ghostlie beholding with everlasting marvailing in this high over-passing unmeasurable love that our Lord hath to us of his goodnes.

And therefore, we may aske of our Lover with reverence, all that we will: for our kindlie will is to have God, and the goodwill of God is to have us: and we may never cease of willing, ne of loving, till we have him in fulhead of joy.

And then we may no more will; for he will that we be occupied in knowing and loving, till the time cometh that we shall be fulfilled in heaven.

And therefore was this lesson of love shewed with all that followeth as you shall see; for the strength and the ground of all was shewed in the first sight: for of all things, the beholding and the loving of the Maker, maketh the soul to seem least in his own sight, and most filleth it with reverent dread and true meekness, and with plenty of charity to his even Christian.

The Seventh Chapter.

AND to learn us this as to my understanding, our good Lord shewed our Lady Mary in the same time, that is to mean, the high wisdom and truth that she had in beholding her Maker.

This wisdom and truth made her to behold her God so great, so high, so mighty, and so good. This greatness and this noblety of her beholding of God, fulfilled her of reverend deed: and with this she saw herself so litle and so low, so simple and so poor, in regard of her God, that this reverend dread fulfilled her of meekness. And thus by this ground she was fulfilled of grace, and of all manner of vertues, and passeth all creatures.

And in all the time that he shewed this that I have now said in ghostly sight, I saw the bodily sight, lasting of the plentuous bleeding of the head, the great drops of blood fell down from under the garland like pellots, seeming as it had come out of the veins: and in the coming out they were brown red, for the blood was full thick, and in the spreading abroad they were bright red; and when it came at the brows, there they vanished.

And notwithstanding, the bleeding continued till many

things were seen and understanded; nevertheless, the fair head, and the lively head continued in the same beauty and liveliness.

The plentuous head is like to the drops of water that fall off the evesing of an house after a great shower of rain, that fall so thick, that no man may number them with any bodily wit. And for the roundness, they were like to the seal of her ring in the spreading of the forehead.

These three things came to my mind in the time; pellets, for the roundhead in the comming out of the blood; the scale of herring, for the round-head in the spreading; the dropps of the evesing of an house, for the plentuous head unnumerable.

This shewing was quick and lively, and hideous, and dreadful, and sweet, and lovely. And of all the sight that I saw, this was most comfort to me, that our good Lord that is so reverent and dreadful, is so homely and so courteous: and this most fulfilled me with liking and sickness of soul.

And to the understanding of this, he shewed this open example. '*It is the most worship that a solemn King or a great Lord may do to a poor servant, if he will be homely with him; and namely, if he shew it himself of a full true meaning, and with a glad chere both in private and openly.*' Then thinketh this poor creature thus: 'Lo, what might this noble Lord do more worship and joy to me, than to show to me that am so little; this marvelous homeliness, verily it is more joy and liking to me, than if he gave me great gifts, and were himself strange in manner.'

This bodily example was shewed so high, that this mans heart might be ravished, and almost forget himself for joy of this great homeliness.

Thus it faireth by our Lord Jesu, and by us, for verily it is the most joy that may be as to my sight, that he that is highest and mightest, nobliest and worthiest, is lowest and meekest, homliest and courtesiest. And truly and verily, this marvellous joy shall he shew us all when we shall see him.

And this will our good Lord, that we believe, and trust, joy, and like comfort us, and make solace, as we may with his grace and with his help, into the time that we see it verily; for the most fulhed of joy that we shall have as to my sight, is this marvellous courtesie and homeliness of our Father that is our Maker in our Lord Jesu Christ, that is our Brother and our Saviour.

But this marvelous homlliness may no man know in this life, but if he have it by special shewing of our Lord, or of great plenty of grace inwardly given of the Holy Ghost, but faith and belief with charity deserve the meed, and so it is had by grace.

For in faith, with hope and charity, our life is grounded; the shewing is made to whom that God will plainly teach, the same opened and declared with many privy points belonging to our faith and belief, which be worshipful to be known.

And when the shewing which is given for a time is passed and hid, then faith keepeth it by grace of the Holy Ghost unto our lives end.

And thus by the shewing, it is none other than faith, no less, no more, as it may be seen by our Lords meaning in the same matter, by than it come to the last end.

The Eighth Chapter.

And as long as I saw this sight of the plentuousness of bleeding of the head, I might never stint of these words, *Benedicite Dominus.* In which shewing, I understood six things.

The *first* is, the tokens of the blessedful passion, and the plentuous shedding of his precious blood.

The *second* is, the maiden that is his dear worthy mother.

The *third* is, the blessedful God-head that ever was, and shall be all mighty, all Wisdom, and all Love.

The *fourth* is, all thing that he hath made: for well I wote that heaven and earth, and all that is made, is great, large, fair and good: but the cause why it sheweth so litle to my sight, was, for I saw it in the presence of him that is the Maker; for a soul that seeth the Maker of all thing, all that is made seemeth full litle.

The *fifth* is, that he that made all thing that is made for love, and by the same love it is kept, and shall be without end, as it is before said.

The *sixth* is, that God is all thing that is good, as to my sight; and the goodness that all thing hath, it is he.

And all this our Lord shewed in the first sight, and gave me space and time to behold it; and the bodily sight stinted, and the ghostly sight dwelleth in my understanding. And I abode with reverent dread, joying in that I saw, and desiring, as I durst, to see more if it were his will, or longer time the same sight.

In all this I was much stirred in charity to mine even Christian, that they might all see and know the same that I saw; for I would that it were comfort to them, for all this sight was shewed in general. Then said I to them that were with me, 'It is this day, dooms-day with me.'

And this I said, for I went to have died: for that day that man or woman dieth, is he deemed particularly, as he shall be without end, as to my understanding.

This I said, for I would they should love God the better, for to make them to have mind that this life is short, as they might see in example; for in all this time I weened to have dyed, and that was marvaile to me, and wonder in party; for methought this vision was shewed for them that should live: all that I say of me, I mean in person of all my even Christian; for I am learned in the ghostly shewing of our Lord God that he meaneth so.

And therefore, I pray you all for God's sake, and counsel you for your own profit, that you leave the beholding of a wretch, that it was shewed to; and mightily, wisely, and meekly, behold in God, that of his courtesie, love, and endless goodness, would shew it generally in comfort of us all: for it is Gods will that ye take it with a great joy and liking, as Jesu Christ hath shewed it to you.

The Ninth Chapter.

For the shewing I am not good; but if I love God the better, and in asmuch as ye love God the better, it is more to you than to me.

I say not this to them that be wise, for they wit it well, but I say it to you that be simple, for ease and comfort; for we be all one in love: for verily it was not shewed to me, for that God loveth me better than the least soul that is in grace: for I am sure, there be many that never hath shewing ne sight but of the common teaching of Holy Church, that love God better than I: for if I look singularly to myself, I am right nought; but in general I am I hope in one-head of charity with all my even Christian; for in this one head standeth the life of all mankind that shall be saved; for God is all that is good as to my sight.

And God hath made all that is made, and God loveth all that he hath made; and he that generally loveth all his even Christen, for God he loveth all that is.

For in mankind that shall be saved, is comprehended all; that is to say, all that is made, and the Maker of all; for in man is God, and in God is all; and he that loveth thus, he loveth all.

And I hope by the grace of God, he that beholdeth it thus, shall be truly taught, and mightily comforted, if him needeth comfort: I speak of them that shall be saved, for in this time God shewed me none other.

But in all thing I believe as Holy Church preacheth and teacheth; for the faith of Holy Church, which I had before hand understanding, and as I hope by the grace of God will fully keep it in use and custome, stood continually in my sight, willing and meaning never to receive any thing that might be contrary thereto. And with this intent, and with this meaning I beheld the shewing with all my diligence; for in all this blessed shewing, I beheld it as in Gods meaning.

All this was shewed by three parts; that is to say, by bodily sight, and by words formed in my understanding, and by ghostly sight; but the ghostly sight I cannot, ne may shew it as openly, ne as fully as I would; but I trust in our Lord God Almighty, that he shall of his goodness, and for your love, make you to take it more ghostly and more sweetly than I can or may tell it.

The Second Revelation.

The Tenth Chapter.

AND after this, I saw with bodily sight, in the face of the crucifix that hung before me: in the which, I beheld continually a part of his passion; despite, spitting, sulloing and buffeting, and many languring pains, more that I can tell; and often changing of colour: and one time I saw how half the face, beginning at the ear, over yede with dry blood, till it closed into the mid-face: and after that, the other half be closed in the same wise. And the whiles, it vanished in this party even as it came.

This saw I bodily sweinly and darkly; and I desired more bodily light to have seen more clearly, and I was answered in my reason, '*If God will shew thee more, he shall be thy light, thou need none but him.*'

For I saw him and sought him: for we be now so blind and so unwise, that we can never seek God till what time that he of his goodness sheweth him to us. And when we see ought of him graciously, then are we stirred by the same grace, to seek with great desire to see him more blessedfully. And thus I saw him and sought him, and I had him and wanted him: and this is and should be our common working in this life, as to my sight.

One time my understanding was litle down into the sea-ground; and there saw I hills, and dales green, seeming as it were most begrowing with wrake and gravel: then I understood thus, that if a man or woman were there under the broad water, and he might have sight of God, so as God is with a man continually, he should be safe in soul and body, and take no harm, and overpassing, he should have more solace and comfort than all this world may or can tell.

For he will that we believe that we see him continually, though that us think that it be but litle, and in the belief he maketh us evermore to get grace; for he will be seen, and he will be sought, and he will be abiden, and he will be trusted.

This second shewing was so low, and so litle, and so simple, that my spirits were in great travail in the beholding, mourning, dreadful, and longing; for I was sometime in a fear, whether it was a shewing or none; and then divers times our Lord gave me more sight, whereby that I understood truly, that it was a shewing.

It was a figure and a likeness of our foul black deeds, which our fair bright blessed Lord bare for our sin. It made me to think of the Holy Vernacle of Rome, which he protraid with his own blessed face, when he was in his hard passion, wilfully going to his death, and often changing of colour, of the brown head, and the black-head, rewlyhead and lean-head.

Of this image many marvelled how that might be standing, that he protraid it with his blessed face, which is the fairest of heaven, flower of earth, and the fruit of the Maidens womb. Then how might this image be so discoloured and so far from fair-head, I desire to see as I have understood by the grace of God.

We know in our faith and in our belief, by the teaching and preaching of Holy Church, that the blessedfull Trinity made mankind to his image and likeness: in the same manner wise we know, that when man fell so deep and so wretchedly by sin, there was none other help to restore man but through him that made man.

And he that made man for love, by the same love he would restore man to the same bliss and over-passing.

And right as we were made like to the Trinity in our first making, our Maker would that we should be like to Jesu Christ our Saviour in heaven without end by the vertue of our own making.

Then between these two he would for love, and for worship of man, make himself as like to man in this deadly life, in our foul-head and in our wretchedness, as man might be without guilt: whereof it meaneth as is before said, it was the image and the likeness of our foul black deeds, wherein our fair bright blessed Lord hid his God-head.

But verily I dare say, and we ought to believe, that so

fair a man was never none but he, till what time that his fair colour was changed with travaile and sorrow, passion and dying.

Of this it speaketh in the Second Revelation, and in the xviii[th] chapter, where it speaketh more of the same likeness. And there it saith of the Vernacle of Rome, it meaneth by diverse changing of colour, and either sometime more comfortable and lively, and sometime more ruful and deadly, as it may be seen hereafter; and this vision was a learning to my understanding, that the continually seeking of the soul pleaseth God much; for it may do no more than seek, suffer, and trust.

And this is wrought in every soul that hath it by the Holy Ghost.

And the clearness of finding it, is of the special grace, when it is his will; the seeking with faith, hope, and charity, pleaseth our Lord; and the finding, pleaseth the soul, and fulfilleth it with joy.

And thus was I learned to my understanding, that seeking is as good as beholding, for the time that he will suffer the soul to be in travaile. It is Gods will that we seek into the beholding of him; for by that shall he shew us himself of his special grace, when he will.

And how a soul shall have her in his beholding, he shall teach himself, and that is most worship to him, and most profit to the soul, and most received of meekness and vertues, with the grace and leading of the Holy

Ghost; for a soul that only resigneth him to God with very trust, either in seeking or in beholding, it is the most worship that he may do, as to my sight.

These be two workings that may be seen in this vision: that one is *seeking*, the other is *beholding*. The *seeking* is common, that each soul may have with his grace, and ought to have discretion and teaching of Holy Church.

It is God's will that we have *three* things in our seeking of his gift. The *first* is, that we seek wilfully and busily without sloath, as it may be with his grace, gladly and merrily, without unreasonable heaviness and vain-sorrow. The *second*, that we abide him stedfastly for his love, without grudging and striving against him, into lives end, for it shall last but a while. The *third* is, that we trust in him mightily of full .and true faith: for it is his will that we know, that he shall appear suddenly and blessedfully to all his lovers.

For his working is privy, and he will be perceived; and his appearing shall be sweet, sudden; and he will be trusted, for he is full homely, curteous. Blessed mote he be.

The Third Revelation.

The Eleventh Chapter.

And after this, I saw God in a point; that is to say, in my understanding: by which sight I saw that he is in all thing. I beheld with advisement, seeing and knowing in that sight, that he doth all that is done. I marvelled in that sight with a soft dread, and thought what is sin; For I saw truly, that God doth all thing, be it never so litle. And I saw verily, that nothing is done by happ, ne by adventure, but all by the aforesaid wisdom of God; if it be happ or adventure in the sight of man, our blindhead and un-fore-sight is the cause. For those things that be in the foresaid wisdom of God, been fro without beginning, which rightfully and worshipfully continually he leadeth to the best end: as it cometh about falling to us suddenly, our unwitting. And thus by our blindness, and our unforesight, we say these things be by happs and adventure.

Thus I understand in this shewing of love: for well I wot in the sight of our Lord God, is no happ, ne adventure. Wherefore me behoved needs to grant, that all things that are done, are well done; for our Lord God doth all: for in this time the working of creatures was not shewed, but of our Lord God in the creatures; for he is in the mid point of all things, and all he doth. And I am sure that he doth no sin.

And here I saw verily that sin is no deed; for in all this, sin was not shewed. And I would no longer marvel in this, but beheld our Lord what he would shew.

And thus as it might be for the time, the rightfulness of God's work was shewed for the soul.

Rightfulness hath two fair properties. It is *right*, and it is *full:* and so be all the works of our Lord. And thereto needeth neither working of mercy ne grace: for they be all rightful, wherein faileth right nought. And in an other time, he shewed for beholding of sin naked as I shall say. After when he useth working of mercy and of grace: this vision was shewed to my understanding; for our Lord will have the soul turned truly unto the beholding of him, and generally of all his works, for they be full good. And all his dooms be easie and sweet, and two great eyes bringing the soul that is turned from the beholding of the blind deeming of man, into the faire sweet deeming of our Lord God. For man, he holdeth some deeds well done, and some deeds evil: and our Lord beholdeth them not so, for as all that hath being in kind is of God's making, so is all thing that is done in property of God's doing. For it is easie to understand that the best deed is well done; and so well as the best deed that is done, and the highest, so well is the least deed done: and all in the property and in the order that our Lord hath it ordeined tofore without beginning. For there is no Door but he.

I saw full truly, that he changed never his purpose in no manner of thing, ne never shall without end: for there was nothing unknown to him in his rightful ordinance fro without beginning. And therefore all thing were set in order ere anything was made, as it should stand without end; and no manner of thing shall fail of that point; for he hath made all thing in fulhead of goodness.

And therefore the blessed Trinity is ever full pleased in all his works. And all this shewed he full blessedly, meaning thus, '*See I am God: See I am in all things: See I do all things: See I never left my hands of my works, ne never shall without end: See I lead all thing to the end that I ordaine it to, for without beginning, by the same might, wisdom, and love, that I made it with, How should anything be amiss?*' Thus mightily, wisely, and lovingly was the soul examined in this vision. Then saw I verily that me behoveth needs to assent with great reverence and joy in God.

The Fourth Revelation.

The Twelfth Chapter.

AND after this I saw beholding the body plentuously bleeding, in seeming of the scourging, as thus: the fair skin was broken full deep into the tender flesh, with sharp smitings, all about the sweet body: the hot blood ran out so plenteously, that there was neither seen skin, ne wound, but as it were all blood. And when it came where it should have fallen down, there it vanished: notwithstanding the bleeding continued a while, till it might be seen with advisement. And this was so plentuous to my sight, that me thought if it had been so in kind and in substance for that time, it should have made the bed all on blood, and have passed over all about.

Then came to my mind, that God hath made waters plentuous in earth to our service, and to our bodily ease, for tender love that he hath to us. But yet liketh him better, that we take full holsomely his blessed blood to wash us from sin, for there is no liquor that is made that liketh him so well to give us: for it is most plentuous, as it is most precious, and that by the vertue of the blessed Godhead, and it is our own kind, and blessedfully overfloweth us by the vertue of his precious love.

The dear worthy blood of our Lord Jesu Christ, also verily as it is most precious, as verily it is most plentuous. Behold and see the vertue of this precious plenty of his dear worthy blood. It descended down into hell, and brake her bonds, and delivered them all that were there which belongeth to the court of heaven. The precious plenty of his dear worthy blood overfloweth all earth, and is ready to wash all creatures of sin which be of good-will, have been, or shall be. The precious plenty of his dear worthy blood ascendeth up into heaven in the blessed body of our Lord Jesu Christ: and there is in him bleeding, praying for us to the Father, and is and shall be as long as us needeth. And evermore it floweth in all heaven, enjoying the salvation of all mankind that be there, and shall be fulfilling the number that faileth.

The Fifth Revelation.

The Thirteenth Chapter.

And after, or that God shewed any words, he suffered me to behold him a conveniable time: and all that I had seen and all the understanding that was therein, as the simpleness of the soul might take it.

Then he without voyce and opening of lips formed in my soul these words, '*Herewith is the fiend overcome.*' This word said our Lord, meaning his blessed passion, as he shewed before. In this our Lord shewed a part of the fiends malice, and fully his unmight, for he shewed that the passion of him is the overcoming of the fiend. God shewed that the fiend hath now the same malice that he had before the incarnation; and also sore he travelleth: and as continually he seeth, that all souls of salvation escape him worshipfully by the vertue of his precious passion, and that is his sorrow, and full evil is he ashamed. For all that God suffereth him to do turneth us to joy, and him to shame and pain. And he hath as much sorrow when God giveth him leave to work, as when he worketh not; and that is, for he may never do as ill as he would, for his might is all locked in God's hand; but in God may be no wrath as to my sight. For our good Lord endlesly having regard to his own worship, and to the profit of all them that shall be saved with might and right, he withstandeth the reproved, the which of malice and of shrewdness busie them to contrary, and do against God's will.

Also I saw our Lord scorning his malice, and naughting his unmight: and he will that we do so. For this sight I laught mightly, and that made them to laugh that were about me, and their laughing was a liking to me: I thought that I would that all my even Christen had seen as I saw, then should all they have laughed with me; but I saw not Christ laughing. But well I wot that sight that he shewed me, made me to laugh: for I understood that we may laugh in comforting of our self, and joying in God, for the fiend is overcome. And there I saw him scorn his malice; it was beholding to my understanding into our Lord; that is to say, an inward shewing of sooth fastness without changing of cheere: for as to my sight it is a worshipful property that is in God, which is durable.

And after this I fell into a sadness, and said, 'I see three things, game, scorn, and earnest. I see game, that the fiend is overcome: and I see scorne, that God scorneth him, and he shall be scorned: and I see earnest, that he is overcome by the blessedful passion and death of our Lord Jesu Christ, that was done in full great earnest, and with sad travel.' And there I said that he is scorned; I meant that God scorneth him, that is to say, for he seeth him now as he shall do without end; for in this God shewed that the fiend is damned. And this meant I, there I said he should be scorned: for I saw he shall be scorned at doomes-day generally of all that shall be saved, to whose salvation he hath had great envy; for then he shall see that all the woe and tribulation that he hath done them, shall be turned into encrease of their joy without end. And all the pain and the sorrow that he would have brought them to, shall for ever go with him to hell.

The Sixth Revelation.

The Fourteenth Chapter.

AND after this our Lord said, '*I thank thee of thy service, and of thy travel of thy youth.*' And in this my understanding was lift up into heaven, where I saw our Lord God as a lord in his own house, which lord hath called all his dear worthy friends to a solemn feast. Then I saw the Lord taking no place in his own house; but I saw him royally reign in his house, and all fulfilleth it with joy and mirth, endlesly to glad and solace his dear worthy friends, full homely and full curteously with marvelous melody in endless love, in his own fair blessedful cheer: which glorious cheer of the Godhead fulfilleth all heaven of joy and bliss. God shewed *three degrees* of bliss that each soul shall have in heaven, that willingfully hath served God in any degree in earth. The *first* is, the worship and thanks that he shall receive of our Lord God when he is delivered of paine: this thanks is so high and so worshipful, that him thinketh that it filleth him, though there were no more; for methought all the pain and travel that might be suffered of all living men, might not have deserved the worshipful thank that one man shall have that wilfully hath served God. For the *second*, that all the blessed creatures that be in heaven, shall see the worshipful thanking: and he maketh his service known to all that be in heaven. And in this time this example was shewed, a king, if he thank his subjects, it is a great worship to them, and if he make it known to all the realm, then their worship is much encreased. And for the *third*, that as new, and as liking as it is undertaken that time, right so shall it last without end. And I saw that homely and sweetly was this shewed, that the age of every man shall be known in heaven, and be rewarded for his wilful service, and for his time; and namely the age of them that wilfully and freely offer their youth to God, passingly is rewarded, and wonderfully thanked; for I saw that when or what time that a man or woman be truly turned to God, for one dayes service, and for his endless will, he shall have all these three degrees of bliss. And the more that the loving soul seeth this courtesie of God, the levir she is to serve him all her life.

The Seventh Revelation.

The Fifteenth Chapter.

AND after this, he shewed a sovereign ghostly liking in my soul: in this likeing, I was fulfilled of everlasting sureness, mightily fastned without any painful dread. This feeling was so glad and so ghostly, that I was all in peace, in ease and in rest, that there was nothing in earth that should have grieved me. This lasted but a while, and I was turned and left to myself in heaviness, and weariness of my life, and irkeness of my self, that unneth I could have patience to live: there was no comfort, ne none to ease my feeling, but faith, hope, and charity: and these I had in truth, but full litle in feeling.

And none after this our blessed Lord gave me again of the comfort and the rest in soul, likeing and sureness, so blessedfully and so mightifully, that no dread, ne sorrow, ne no pain bodily, ne ghostly that might be suffered should have diseased me. And then the pain sheweth again to my feeling, and then the joy and the liking: and now that one, and now that other divers times; I suppose about twenty times. And in the time of joy, I might have said with Saint Paul, 'Nothing shall depart me fro the charity of Christ.' And in the pain I might have said with Saint Peter, 'Lord save me, I perish.'

This vision was shewed to learn me at my understanding, that it is speedful to some souls to feel on this wise. Sometime to be in comfort, and sometime to fail, and to be left to themself; God will that we know that he keepeth us ever in like sure, in woe, and in weale. And for profit of mans soul, a man is sometimes left to himself, although his sin is not ever the cause; for in this time I sinned not, wherefore I should be left to myself, for it was so sudden. Also, I deserved not to have had this blessedful feeling, but freely our Lord giveth it when he will; and suffereth us in woe sometime, and both is one love. For it is Gods will that we hold us in comfort with all our might; for bliss is lasting without end, and pain is passing, and shall be brought to naught to them that shall be saved. Therefore it is not God's will, that we follow the feeling of pains in sorrow and mourning for them, but suddenly pass over, and hold us in the endless liking that is God.

The Eighth Revelation.

And the Sixteenth Chapter.

AFTER this, Christ shewed a part of his passion, near his dying: I saw the sweet face as it were dry and bloodless, with pale dying, and dead pale languring, and then turned more dead into blew, and after in brown-blew, as the flesh turned more deep dead. For his passion shewed to me most properly in his blessed face, and namely in his lips; therein I saw these four colours; those that were before fresh and ruddy, lively and liking to my sight. This was a pittiful changing, to see this deep dying; and also his most cloggering together and dried to my sight. And the sweet body waxed brown and black, all changed and turned out of the fair, fresh, and lively colour of himself, into dry dying; for that same time that our blessed Saviour dyed upon the roode, it was a dry sharp wind, wonder could, as to my sight: and what time that the precious blood was bled out of the sweet body that might pass therefro, yet there was a moisture in the sweet flesh of Christ, as it was shewed. Bloodshed and pain dried within, and blowing of the wind and cold, coming from without met together in the sweet body of Christ: and these four dryed the flesh of Christ by process of time. And though this pain were bitter and sharp, yet it was full long lasting, as to my sight. And the pain dried up all the lively spirits of Christs flesh. Thus I saw the sweet flesh dry in my sight, part after part drying with marvellous pain; and as long as any spirit had life in Christs flesh, so long suffered he. This long pain seemed to me as if he had been a sennet dead, dying at the point of out-passing, always suffering the great pain: and there I saw it seemed as he had been a sennet dead: it specifieth, that the sweet body was so discoloured, so dry, so clongen, so deadly, and so piteous, as he had been sevenight dead, continually dying. And methought the drying of Christs flesh was the most pain, and the last of his passion.

The Ninth Revelation.

And the Seventeenth Chapter.

AND in this drying, was brought to my mind this word that Christ said, '*I thirst.*' For I saw in Christ a double thirst, one bodily, and another ghostly. This word was shewed for the bodily thirst: and for the ghostly thirst was shewed as I shall say after. And I understood by the bodily thirst, that the body had feeling of moisture;

for the blessed flesh and bones was left all alone without blood and moisture. The blessed body dried all alone long time with wringing of the nails and weight of the body; for I understood that for tenderness of the sweet hands, and the sweet feet, by the great hardness and grievousness of the nails, the wounds waxed wide, and the body setled for weight by long time hanging, and pearcing and raising of the head, and binding of the crown, all baken with dry blood, with the sweet hair clinging the dry flesh to the thorns, and the thorns to the flesh drying: and in the beginning while the flesh was fresh and bleeding, the continual setting of the thorns made the wounds wide. And furthermore, I saw, that the sweet skin, and the tender flesh, with the hair, and with the blood, was all raced and loosed about with the thorns, and broken in many pieces, and were hanging as they would hastily have fallen down while it had kind moisture; how it was down I saw not, but I understood that it was with the sharp thorns, and the boystrous grievous sitting on of the garland, not sparing, and without pity, that altho brake the sweet skin with the flesh, and the hair loosed it from the bone; where through it was broken in pieces as a cloath, and sagging downward, as it would hastily have fallen for heaviness and for looseness. And that was great sorrow and dread to me, for methought that I would not for my life have seen it fall.

This continued a while, and after it began to change;

and I beheld and marvelled how it might be, and then I saw it was, for it began to dry, and stint a part of the weight that was round about the garland. And so it was invironed all about, as it were garland upon garland; the garland of thornes was dyed with the garland of blood, and that other garland and the head all was one colour as clottered blood when it was dried. The skin and the flesh that seemed of the face and of the body, was small rimpild with a tawny colour, like a dry board when it is aged, and the face more brown than the body. I saw *four* manner of drying: the *first* was bloodless; the *second*, pain following after; the *third* is, that he was hanging up in the aire, as men hang a cloath for to dry; the *fourth*, that the bodily kind asked liquor, and there was no manner of comfort ministred to him. Ah, hard and grievous was that pain, but much more hard and grievous it was when the moisture failed, and all began to dry thus clinging. These were two pains that shewed in the blessed head: the first wrought to the drying while it was moist, and that other slow, with clinging and drying, with blowing of wind from without; that dryed him more, and pained with cold, than my heart can think, and all other pains, for which pains I saw, that all is too litle that I can say, for it may not be told. The shewing of Christs pains filled me full of pains, for I wist well that he suffered but once; but as he would shew it me, and fill me with mind, as I had before desired. And in all this time of Christs presence, I felt no pain but for Christs pains.

Then thought me, I knew full litle what pain it was that I asked, and as a wretch I repented me, thinking if I had wist what it had been, loath had me been to have prayed it, for methought my pains passed any bodily death. I thought, 'Is any pain in hell like this?' and I was answered in my reason, '*Hell is an other pain, for their is despair; but of all pains that lead to salvation, this is the most, to see the Lover to suffer.*' How might any pain be more than to see him that is all my life, all my bliss, and all my joy, suffer? Here left I stedfastly, that I loved Christ so much above my self, that there was no pain that might be suffered, like to that sorrow that I had to see him in pain.

The Eighteenth Chapter.

HERE I saw in part the compassion of our blessed lady Saint Mary, for Christ. And she was so onyd in love, that the greatness of her love was cause of the greatness of her pain; for in this I saw a substance of kind love continued by grace, that his creatures have to him; which kind love was most fulsomelie shewed in his sweet mother, and overpassing: for so much as she loved him more than all other, her pain passed all other; for ever the higher, the mightier; the sweeter that the love is, the more sorrow it is to the Lover to see that body in pain that he loved. And so all his disciples, and all his true lovers suffered more pain than their own bodily dying: for I am sure by my own feeling, that the least of them loved him so far above himself, that it passeth all that I can say.

Here saw I a great oning between Christ and us, to my understanding; for when he was in pain we were in pain, and all creatures that might suffer pain, suffered with him; that is to say, all creatures that God hath made to our service. The firmament and earth failed for sorrow in their kind, in the time of Christs dying; for it longeth kindly to their property to know him for their Lord, in whom all their vertue standeth. And when he feeled, then behoved needs to them for kindness to feel with him, in as much as they might, for sorrow of his pains. And thus they that were his friends suffered pain for love. And generally, all that is to say, they that knew him not, suffered for feeling of all manner of comfort save the mighty privy keeping of God. I mean of two manner of people that know him not, as it may be understood by two persons: that one was Pilate, that other person was St. Dionise of France, which was that time a Paynius; for when he saw wonders and marveils, sorrows and dreads that befell at that time, he said, "Either the world is now at an end, or else, he that is maker of kinds suffereth." Wherefore he did write on an altar, 'This is an altar of the unknown God.' God of his goodness, that maketh plannets, and the elements to work in their kind to the blessed man, and to the cursed. In that time it was withdrawn from both: wherefore it was, that they that knew him not were in sorrow that time. Thus was our Lord Jesu pained for us, and we stand all in this manner of pain with him, and shall do till that we come to his bliss, as I shall say hereafter.

The Nineteenth Chapter.

In this time I would have looked fro the cross, and I durst not; for I wist well whiles that I beheld the cross I was sure and safe. Therefore I would not assent to put my soul in peril, for besides, the cross was no sureness for dreed of fiends. Then had I a proffer in my reason, as it had been friendly said to me, '*Look up to heaven to his Father.*' And then saw I well with the faith that I felt, that there was nothing between the cross and heaven that might have diseased me. Here me behoved to look up, or else to answer; I answered inwardly with all the might of my soul, and said, 'Nay, I may not, for thou art my heaven.' This I said, for that I would not; for I had leaver have been in that pain till dooms-day, than have come to heaven otherwise than by him; for I wist well that he that bound me so sore, he should unbind me when he would. Thus was I learned to choose Jesu for my heaven, whom I saw only in pain at that time: me liked no other heaven than Jesu, which shall be my bliss when I come there; and this hath ever been a comfort to me, that I chose Jesu to be my heaven by his grace, in all this time of passion and sorrow. And that hath been a learning to me that I should evermore do so, to chose Jesu only to my heaven in weal and in woe. And though I as a wretch hath repented me; as I said before; if I had wist what pain it had been, I had been loath to have prayed it; here I saw verily that it was grudging and frailty of the flesh without assent of the soul in which God assigneth no blame. Repenting and wilful choise be two contraries, which I felt both at that time. And those be two parts, that one outward, that other inward. The outward party is our deadily flesh, which is now in pain, and now in woe, and shall be in this life: whereof I felt much at this time; and that part was that I repented. The inward party is a high and a blessedful life, which is all in peace and love: and this is more privily felt; and this party is in which mightily, wisely, and wilfully I chose Jesu to my heaven. And in this I saw truly, that the inward party is master and soveraign to the outward, nought charging nor taking heede to the wills of that; but all the intent, and the will is set endless to be oned to our Lord Jesu: that the outward party should draw the inward to assent, was not shewed to me, but that the inward party draweth the outward party by grace, and both shall be owned in bliss without end by the vertue of Christ, this was shewed.

The Twentieth Chapter.

AND thus saw I our Lord Jesu languring long time for the uning of the God-head, gave strength to the man-head for love, to suffer more than all men might; I mean not only more pain than all men might suffer, but also, that he suffered more pain than all man of salvation that ever was from the first beginning into the last day, might tell or fully think. Having regard to the worthiness of the highest worshipful King, and the shameful and despiteous painful death; for he that is highest and worthiest, was foulest condemned and utterly despised: for his passion is to think and to know that he is God that suffered. Seeing after these other two points which be lower; that one is what he suffered; and that other for whom that he suffered. And in this he brought to mind in part the height, and the nobility of the glorious God-head, and therewith the precious head and the tenderness of the blessedful body which be together owned, and also the loathfulness that in our kind is to suffer pain; for asmuch as he was most tender and clean, right, so he was most strong and mighty to suffer: and for every mans sin that shall be saved he suffered; and every mans sorrow, dissolation and anguish he saw, and sorrowed for kindness and love; for in as much as our Lady sorrowed for his pains, as much suffered he sorrow for her sorrows. And moreover in as much as the sweet man-head of him was worthier in kind; for as long as he was passible, he suffered for us, and sorrowed for us. And now he is up-risen, and no more passible; yet he suffered with us, as I shall say after. And I beholding all this by his grace, saw that the love in him was so strong which he hath to our soul, that willingfully he chose it with great desire; and mildly he suffered it with great joy; for the soul that he beholdeth thus, when it is touched by grace he shall verily see that the pains of Christs passion pass all pains; that is to say, which pains shall be turned into everlasting joy by the vertue of Christs passion. It is Gods will as to my understanding that we have *three* manners of beholding of his blessed passion. The *first* is the beholding the hard pain that he suffered with a contrition and compassion: and that shewed our Lord in this time, and gave me might and grace to see it. And I looked after the departing with all my mights, and wende to have seen the body all dead; but I saw him not so: and right in the same time that me thought by seeming that the life might no longer last, and the shewing of the end behoved needs to be nigh,

The Twenty-first Chapter.

SUDDENLY I beholding in the same cross, he changed in blessedful chear; the changing of his blessed chear changed mine; and I was as glad and merry as it was possible. Then brought our Lord merrily to my mind, '*Where is now any point of thy pain or of thy anguish?*' And I was full merry; I understood that we be now in our Lords meaning, in his cross with him; in our pains, and in our passion dying. And we wilfully abiding in the same cross, with his help and his grace into the last point; suddenly he shall change his chear to us: and we shall be with him in heaven; between that one and that other shall all be one time; and then shall all be brought into joy. And so meant he in this shewing, '*Where is now any point of thy pain or of thy grief?*' And we shall be full of bliss; and here saw I verily, that if he shewed now to us his blessedful chear, there is no pain in earth, ne in no other place that should trouble us: but all things should be to us joy and bliss; but for he sheweth us the sad chear of passion, as he bare in this life his cross; therefore we be in disease and travaile with him as our kind asketh. And the cause why that he suffereth, is, for he will of his goodness make us the heirs with him in his bliss. And for this litle pain that we suffer here, we shall have an high endless knowing in God, which we might never have without that; and the harder our pains have been with him in his cross, the more shall our worship be with him in his kingdom.

The Twenty-second Chapter.

THEN said our good Lord asking, '*Art thou well apaid that I suffered for thee?*' I said, 'yea good Lord gramercy; yea good Lord blessed mote thou be.' Then said Jesu our good Lord, '*If thou art apaid, I am apaid: It is a joy, a bliss, an endless liking to me, that ever I suffered passion for thee: and if I might have suffered more, I would have suffered more.*' In this feeling my understanding was lifted up into heaven: and there I saw *three* heavens; of which sight I was greatly marvelled, and thought I see *three* heavens, and all of the blissedful man-head of Christ; and none is more, none is less, none is higher, none is lower, but even like of bliss. For the *first* heaven, Christ shewed me his Father, in no bodily likeness, but in his property, and in his working; that is to say, I saw in Christ that the Father is. The working of the Father is this, that he giveth meed to his Son Jesu Christ: this gift and this meed is so blissedful to Jesu, that his Father might have given him no meed that might have been liked to him better. For the *first* heaven, that is the pleasing of the Father shewed to me as in heaven, and it was full blissedfully; for he is well pleased with all the deeds that Jesu hath done about our salvation: wherefore we be not only his by his buying, but also by the courteous gift of his Father we be his bliss, we be his meed, we be his worship, we be his crown; and this was a singuler marvaile, and a full delectable beholding, that we be his crown. This that I say is so great bliss to Jesu, that he setteth at naught his travel, and his passion, and his cruel and shameful death. And in these words, '*If I might suffer more, I would suffer more,*' I saw truly, that as often as he might die, as often as he would, and love should never let him have rest till he had done it. And I beheld with great diligence, for to wit, how often he would die if he might: and truly the number passed my understanding, and my wits so far that my reason might not, nor could not comprehend it, ne take it. And when he had thus oft died, or should die, yet he would set it at naught for love; for all thinketh him but litle in regard of his love; for though the sweet manhood of Christ might suffer but once, the goodness of him may never cease of profer, every day he is ready to the same if it might be; for if he, said he, would for my love make new heavens, and new earths, it were but litle in regard: for this might he do each day if he would without any travel. But for to die for my love so often that the number passeth creatures reason, this is the highest profer that our Lord God might make to mans soul, as to my sight. Then meaneth he thus; '*How should it then be, that I should not for thy love do all that I might, which deed grieveth me nought, sithen that I would for thy love dye so often, having no regard to my hard pains?*' And here saw I for the second beholding in his blessed passion, the love that made him to suffer, it passeth as far all his pains, as heaven is above earth; for the pain was a noble, precious, and worshipful deed, done in a time by the working of love: and love was without beginning, is and shall be without end; for which love, he said full sweetly this word: '*If I might suffer more, I would suffer more.*' He said not if it were needful to suffer more; but, '*If I might suffer more.*' For though it were not needful, and he might suffer more, he would. This deed and this work about our salvation, was ordained as well as God might ordaine it; it was done as worshipfully as Christ might do it; and herein I saw a full bliss in Christ; for his bliss should not have been full, if it might any better have been done than it was done.

The Twenty-third Chapter.

AND in these *three* words: '*It is a joy, a bliss, and endless liking to me,*' were shewed *three* heavens, as thus; For the joy, I understood the pleasaunce of the Father; and for the bliss, the worship of the Son; and for the endless liking, of the Holy Ghost. The Father is pleased, the Son is worshipped, and the Holy Ghost liketh. And here saw I for the *third*, beholding in his blessedful passion; that is to say, the joy and the bliss that maketh him to like it: for our courteous Lord shewed his passion to me in five manners; Of which the *first* is, the bleeding of the head; the *second*, discolouring of his blessed face; the *third* is, the plentuous bleeding of the body in seeming of scourging; the *fourth* is, the deep drying; these four as it is before said for the pains of the passion. And the *fifth* is, that was shewed for the joy and the bliss of the passion; for it is Gods will that we have true liking with him in our salvation. And therein he will, that we be mightily comforted and strengthened. And thus will hee merely with his grace, that our soul be occupied; for we be his bliss, for in us he liketh without end. And so shall we in him with his grace; all that he doth for us and hath done, and ever shall, was never cost, ne charge to him, ne might be; but only that he died in our man-head, beginning at the sweet incarnation, and lasting to the blessed uprising on Easter morrow: so long dured the cost and charge about our redemption in deed: in which deed he ever joyeth endlesly, as it is before said. Ah Jesu, will we take heed to this bliss, that is in the blissedful Trinity of our salvation; and that we desire to have asmuch ghostly liking with his grace, as it is before said; that is to say, that the liking of our salvation be like to the joy that Christ hath of our salvation, as it may be while we be here. All the Trinity wrought in the passion of Christ, ministering abundance of vertue and plenty of grace to us by him, but only the maidens son suffered, whereof all the blessed Trinity enjoyeth. And this was shewed in this word, '*Art thou well apaid?*' By that other word Christ said, '*If thou art well apaid, I am well apaid;*' as if he had said, '*It is joy and liking enough to me, and I ask not else of thee of my travel, but that I might appay thee.*'

And in this he brought to my mind the property of a glad Giver; ever a glad Giver taketh but litle heed at the thing that he giveth, but all his desire, and all his intent is, to please him, and solace him to whom he giveth it. And if the receiver take the gift gladly and thankfully, than the courteous Giver setteth at naught all his cost, and all his travel, for joy and delight he hath; for he hath pleased and solaced him that he loved. Plentuously and fully was this shewed. Think as wisely of the greatness of this word, *Ever.* For in that was shewed an high knowing of love that he hath in our salvation, with manifold joys that followen of the passion of Christ. *One* is, that he joyeth that he hath done it in deed, and he shall no more suffer: that *other* is, that he hath therewith bought us from endless pains of hell: an *other* is, that he brought us up into heaven, and made us for to be his crown, and his endless bliss.

The Tenth Revelation.

The Twenty-fourth Chapter.

WITH a good chear our good Lord looked into his side, and beheld with joy; and with his sweet looking, he led forth the understanding of his creature by the same wound into his side within. And there he shewed a fair and delectable place, and large enough for all mankind that shall be saved, and rest in peace and in love: and therewith he brought to mind his dear worthy blood, and his precious water which he let pour out for love. And with the sweet beholding he shewed his blessed heart cloven in two; and with his enjoying he shewed to my understanding in part the blessedful Godhead, as far forth as he would at that time strengthen the poor soul for to understand, as it may be said; that is to mean, the endless love that was without beginning, and is, and shall be ever. And with this our good Lord said well blessedfully, '*Low, how I love thee;* as if he had said, '*My darling, behold and see thy Lord thy God that is thy maker, and thy endless joy. See thine own brother, thy Saviour, my child, behold and see what liking and bliss I have in thy salvation: And for my love enjoy with me.*' And also to more understanding, this blessed word was said: '*Loe, how I love thee;*' as if he had said, '*Behold and see that I loved thee so much, or that I died for thee, that I would die for thee. And now I have died for thee, and suffered willingfully that I may: and now is all my bitter pain, and all my hard travel turned to everlasting joy and bliss to me and to thee. How should it now be that thou shouldest any thing pray me that liked me; but if I should full gladly grant it thee, for my liking is thy holiness, and the endless joy and bliss with me.*' This is the understanding simply, as I can say of this blessed word, '*Loe, how I loved thee.*' This shewed our good Lord to make us glad and merry.

The Eleventh Revelation.

And the Twenty-fifth Chapter.

AND with this chear of mirth and joy, our good Lord looked down on the right side, and brought to my mind, where our Lady stood in the time of his passion, and said, "Wilt thou see her?" And in this sweet word, as if he had said, '*I wot well that thou wilt see my blessed mother: for after myself, she is the highest joy that I might shew thee, and most liking and worship to me, and most she is desired to be seen of all my blessed creatures.*' And for the marvellous, high, and singular love that he hath to this sweet maiden, his blessed mother our lady Saint Mary, he sheweth her bliss and joy; as by the meaning of this sweet word, as if he said, '*Wilt thou see how that I love her, that thou might joy with me in the love that I have in her, and she in me?*' And also to more understanding, this sweet word our good Lord speaketh in love to all mankind, that shall be saved, as it were all to one person; as if he said, '*Wilt thou see in her how thou art loved? for thy love I have made her so high, so noble, so worthy: and this liketh me; and so will I that it do thee.*'

For after himself she is the most blessedful sight: but hereof am I not learned to long to see her bodily presence while I am here; but the vertues of her blessedful soul, her truth, her wisdom, her charity, whereby I am learned to know myself, and reverently dread my God. And when our good Lord had shewed this, and said this word, '*Wilt thou see her?*' I answered and said, 'Yea good Lord, grant mercy, yea good Lord if it be thy will.' Oftentimes I prayed this, and I went to have seen her in bodily liking, but I saw her not so. And Jesu in that word shewed me a ghostly sight of her right; as I had seen her before litle and simple; right so he shewed her then high and noble, and glorious, and pleasing to him above all creatures; and so he will that it be known, that all those that like in him, should also like in her.

And to more understanding he shewed this example; as if a man love a creature singularly above all creatures, he will make all other creatures to love and to like that creature that he loveth so much. And in this word that Jesu said, '*Wilt thou see her?*' methought it it was the most liking word that he might give me of her, with the ghostly shewing that he gave me of her. For our Lord shewed me nothing in special, but our lady Saint Mary, and her shewed *three* times. The *first* was as she conceived; the *second* as she was in her sorrow under the cross; and the *third* was, as she is now in liking, worship, and joy.

The Twelfth Revelation.

The Twenty-sixth Chapter.

AND after this, our Lord shewed him more glorified as to my sight than I saw him before; wherein I was learned, that our soul shall never have rest till it come into him, knowing that he is full of joy, homely and courteous, and blessedful, and very life. Oftentimes our Lord Jesu said, '*I it am, I it am, I it am, That is highest, I it am, that thou lovest, I it am, that thou likest, I it am, that thou servest, I it am, that thou longest I it am, that thou desirest I it am, that thou meanest I it am, that is all I it am, that Holy Church preacheth thee and teacheth thee I it am, that shewed me before to thee.*' The number of thy words passeth my wits and understanding, and all my mights; for they were in the highest as to my sight: for therein is comprehended I cannot tell what; but the joy that I saw in the shewing of them passeth all that heart can think, or soul may desire. And therefore these words be not declared here, but every man after the grace that God giveth him in understanding and longing, receive them in our Lords meaning.

The Thirteenth Revelation.

The Twenty-seventh Chapter.

AND after this our Lord brought to my mind the longing that I had to him before; and I saw nothing letted me but sin. And so I beheld generally in us all; and methought, if sin had not been, we should all have been clean and like to our Lord as he made us. And thus in my folly, before this time, often I wondered why by the great foresaid wisdom of God, the beginning of sin was not letted, for then thought me that all should have been well. This stirring was much to be forsaken; and nevertheless, mourning and sorrow I made therefore, without reason and discretion; but Jesu, that in this vision, informed me of all that me needed, answered by this word, and said, '*Sin is behovely, but all shall be well, and all shall be well, and all manner of thing shall be well.*' In this naked word sin, our Lord brought to my mind generally all that is not good; and the shameful despite, and the uttermost tribulation that he bare for us in this life, and his dying, and all his pains and passion bodily and ghostly, and the pains of all his creatures ghostly and bodily. For we be all in part troubled, and we shall be troubled following our master Jesu, till we be full purged of our deadly flesh, and of all our inward affections, which be not very good. And the beholding of this with all the pains that ever were, or ever shall be. And with all this I understood the passion of Christ, for the most pain and over-passing: and all this was shewed in a touch and readily passed over into comfort; for our good Lord would not that the soul were afraid of this ugly sight, but I saw not sin; for I believe it had no manner of substance, ne no part of being, ne it might not be known but by the pain that is caused thereof: and this pain is something as to my sight for a time, for it purgeth and maketh us to know our self, and ask mercy; for the passion of our Lord is comfort to us against all this, and so is his blessed will; and for the tender love that our good Lord hath to all that shall be saved; he comforteth readily and sweetly, meaning thus: '*It is true, that sin is cause of all this pain; but all shall be well, and all manner of thing shall be well.*' These words were shewed full tenderly, shewing no manner of blame to me, ne to none that shall be safe. Then were it great unkindness of me to blame or wonder on God of my sin, sithen he blameth not me for sin. And in these same words, I saw an high marvellous privity hid in God: which privity, he shall openly make, and shall be known to us in heaven. In which knowing we shall verily see the cause why he suffered sin to come. In which sight, we shall endlesly have joy.

The Twenty-eighth Chapter.

THUS I saw, how Christ hath compassion on us for the cause of sin. And right as I was before in the passion of Christ fulfilled with pain and compassion; like in this I was in party fulfilled with compassion of all my even Christen; for full well he loveth people that shall be saved; that is to say, Gods servants, Holy Church shall be shaked in sorrow, and anguish, and tribulation in this world, as men shaketh a cloath in the wind: and as to this our Lord answered, shewing on this manner; '*Ah, a great thing shall I make hereof in heaven of endless worship, and of everlasting joy.*' Ye, so far forth I saw that our Lord enjoyeth of the tribulation of his servants with pity and compassion; and to each person that he loveth to his bliss, for to bring, he layeth on him something that is no lack in his sight; whereby they be lowed and despised in this world, scorned and mocked, and cast out. And this he doth for to let the harm that they should take of the pomp, and of the pride, and of the vain glory of this wretched life, and make their way ready to come to heaven in bliss without end everlasting. For he saith, '*I shall all to break you from your vain affections, and your vicious pride, and after that I shall gather you, and make you meek and mild, clean and holy by oning to me.'* And then saw I that each kind compassion that man hath on his even Christian with charity; it is Christ in him, that each manner naughting that was shewed in his passion, it was shewed again here in this compassion. Wherein were *two* manner of understandings in our Lords meaning; that *one* was the bliss that we be brought to, wherein he will that we enjoy. That other is for comfort in our pain; for he will that we wit that all shall turn us to worship, and to profit by the vertue of his passion. And that we wit that we suffered right naught alone, but with him, and see him our ground. And that we see his pains and his tribulation pass so far all that we may suffer, that it may not be full thought. And the well beholding of this will save us from grudging and dispair in the feeling of our pains: and if we see verily that our sin deserveth it, yet his love excuseth us, and of his great courtesie he doth away all our blame, and beholdeth us with ruth and pitty, as children, innocents and unloathful.

The Twenty-ninth Chapter.

But in this I stood beholding generally, sweinly and mourningly, saying thus to our Lord in my meaning with full great dreed; 'Ah good Lord, how might all be well for the great harm that is to come by sin to thy creatures?' And here I desired as I durst, to have some more open declaring, wherewith that I might be eased in this. And to this our blessed Lord answered full meekly, and with full lovely cheir; and shewed that Adam's sin was the most harm that ever was done, or ever shall be into the world's end: and also he shewed that this is openly known in all Holy Church in earth. Furthermore, he learned that I should behold the glorious asseethe; for this asseeth-making is more pleasing to the blessed God-head, and more worshipful for man's salvation without comparison, than ever was the sin of Adams harmful. Then meaneth our blessed Lord thus, and in this teaching; that we should take heed to this. '*For sithen that I have made well by the most harm; then it is my will that thou know thereby that I shall make well all that is less.*'

The Thirtieth Chapter.

He gave understanding of *two* parties, *that one* party is our Saviour and our salvation. This blessed part is open, clear, fair, and light, and plenteous for all mankind that is of good will, and that shall be, is comprehended in this part. Hereto we be bound of God, and drawn and counselled, and learned inwardly by the Holy Ghost, and outward by Holy Church in the same grace. In this will our Lord that we be occupied and joying in him, for he joyeth in us: and the more plenteously that we take of this with reverence and meekness, the more thank we deserve of him, and the more speed to our self. And thus may we see and enjoy our part is our Lord. *That other* is hid and sparred from us; that is to say, all that is besides our salvation; for that is our Lord's privy counsel, and it longeth to the royal lordship of God to have his privy counsels in peace. And it longeth to his servants for obedience and reverence not to will to know his counsels. Our Lord hath pity and compassion on us, for that some creatures make them so busie therein; and I am sure if we wist how greatly we should please him, and ease ourself to leave it, we would. The saints in heaven they will nothing wit but what our Lord will shew them; and also their charity and their desire is ruled after the will of our Lord: and thus ought we that our will be like to them; then shall we nothing will, ne desire but the will of our Lord, like as they do; for we be all one in Gods meaning. And here I was learned, that I should only enjoy in our blessed Saviour Jesu, and trust in him for all thing.

The Thirty-first Chapter.

AND thus our good Lord answered to all the questions and doubts that I might make, saying full comfortably: '*I may make all thing well; and I can make all thing well; and I shall make all thing well; and I will make all thing well; and thou shalt see thyself that all manner of thing shall be well.*' There he saith, '*I may,*' I understand for the Father; and there he saith, '*I can,*' I understand for the Son; and there he saith, '*I will,*' I understand for the Holy Ghost; and there he saith '*I shall,*' I understand the unity of the blessed Trinity; three persons and one truth: and there he saith, '*Thou shalt see thyself,*' I understand the coming of all mankind that shall be saved into the blessedful Trinity. And in these five words, God will that we be enclosed in rest, and peace. And thus shall the ghostly thirst of Christ have an end; for this is the ghostly thirst of Christ, the love-longing that lasteth and ever shall, till we see that sight at dooms-day; for we that shall be safe, and shall be Christ's joy and his bliss, been yet here, and some be to come, and so shall some be into that day. Therefore this is his thirst, and love-longing of us all together here in him to our endless bliss, as to my sight; for we be not now fully as whole in him as we shall be then; for we know in our faith, and also it was shewed in all, that Christ Jesu was both God and man: and aneynst the Godhead he is himself highest bliss, and was fro without beginning, and shall be without end: which very endless bliss may never be highed nor lowed in itself. And this was plenteously seen in every shewing, and namely in the xiith. where he saith, '*I it am that is highest.*' And as aneynst Christs manhood; it is known in our faith, and also shewed that he through the vertue of the Godhead, for love to bring us to his bliss suffered pains and passion, and died.

And these be the works of Christs manhood, wherein he enjoyeth. And that shewed he in the ixth where he saith, '*It is a joy, a bliss, and endless liking to me, that ever I suffered passion for thee.*' And this is the bliss of Christs works: and thus he meaneth; there he saith in the same shewing, '*We be his bliss, we be his meed, we be his worship, we be his crown.*' For as aneynst that Christ is our head, he is glorified and unpassible: and as aneynst his body in which all his members be knit, he is not yet full glorified, ne all unpassible: for the same thirst and longing that he had upon the roode-tree, (which desire longing and thirst as to my sight, was in him from without beginning) the same hath he yet, and shall into the time that the last soul that shall be saved, is come up to his bliss. For as truly as there is a property in God of ruth and pity; as verily there is a property in God of thirst and longing: and of the vertue of this longing in Christ, we have to long again to him, without which no soul cometh to heaven. And this property of longing and thirst cometh of the endless goodness of God; right as the property of pity cometh of his endless goodness: and though he have longing and pity, they been sundry properties, as to my sight. And in this standeth the point of ghostly thirst, which is lasting in him as long as we be in need, us drawing up to his bliss. And all this was seen in shewing of compassion, for that shall cease at doomsday. Thus he hath ruth and compassion on us; and he hath longing to have us; but his wisdom and his love suffer not the same to come till the best time.

The Thirty-second Chapter.

ONE time our good Lord said, '*All manner of thing shall be well:*' and another time he said, '*Thou shalt see thy self, that all manner of thing shall be well.*' And in these two the soul took sundry manner of understanding. One was this; that he will, we wit that not only he taketh heed to noble things and to great, but also to litle and to small, to low and to simple, and to one and to other. And so meaneth he in that he saith, '*All manner of thing shall be well;*' for he will that we wit that the least thing shall not be forgotten. Another understanding is this; that there be many deeds evil done in our sight, and so great harms take, that it seemeth to us that it were impossible that ever it should come to a good end. And upon this we look, sorrow and mourn therefore; so that we cannot rest us in the blissedful beholding of God as we should do. And the cause is this; that the use of our reason is now so blind, so low, and so simple, that we cannot know the high marvellous wisdom, the might and the goodness of the blissedful Trinity. And this meaneth he where he saith, '*Thou shalt see thy self, that all manner of thing shall be well.*' As if he said, take now faithfully and trustfully, add at the last end thou shalt be verily in fulhead of joy. And thus in the same five words beforesaid, '*I may make all thing well;*' I understand a mighty comfort of all works of our Lord God that are for to come. There is a deed, the which the blissedful Trinity shall do in the last day, as to my sight: and what the deed shall be, and how it shall be done, it is unknown of all creatures which are beneath Christ, and shall be till when it shall be done. The goodness and the love of our Lord God will, that we wit that it shall be: and the might, and the wisdom of him by the same love will hill it, and hide it from us what it shall be, and how it shall be done. And the cause why he will, we wit it thus is, for he will we be the more eased in our soul, and peaceable in love, leaving the beholding of all tempests that might let us of true enjoying in him.

This is the great deed ordeined of our Lord God fro without beginning, treasured and hid in his blessed breast, only known to himself; by which deed, he shall make all thing well, for right as the blessed Trinity made all thing of naught, right so the same blessed Trinity shall make well all that is not well. And in this sight I marvelled greatly, and beheld our faith, meaning thus; Our faith is grounded in Gods word, and it longeth to our faith, that we believe that Gods word shall be saved in all thing: and one point of our faith is, that many creatures shall be damned, as angels that fell out of heaven for pride, which be now fiends; and many in earth that dyeth out of the faith of Holy Church; that is to say, tho that be heathen: and also many that hath received Christendome, and liveth unchristen life, and so dyeth out of charity; all these shall be damned to hell without end, as Holy Church teacheth me to believe: and standing all this, methought it was unpossible that all manner of thing should be well, as our Lord shewed in this time. And as to this, I had no other answer in shewing of our Lord but this; '*That that is unpossible to thee, is not unpossible to mee; I shall save my word in all thing, and I shall make all thing well.*' And in this I was taught by the grace of God, that I should stedfastly hold me in the faith as I had before understood. And therewith, that I should stand and sadly believe, that all manner thing shall be well, as our Lord shewed in the same time; for this is the great deed that our Lord

God shall do: in which deed he shall save his word in all thing; and he shall make well all that is not well. But what the deed shall be, and how it shall be done, there is no creature beneath Christ that wot it, ne shall wit it till it is done, as to the understanding that I took of our Lords meaning in this time.

The Thirty-third Chapter.

And yet in this I desired as I durst, that I might have some sight of hell, and of purgatory. But it was not my meaning to take proof of any thing that longeth to our faith; for I believed sothfastlie that hell and purgatory is for the same end that Holy Church teacheth for; but my meaning was, that I might have seen for learning in all thing that longeth to my faith, whereby I might live the more to Gods worship, and to my profit. And for ought that I could desire, I ne could see of this right nought, but as it is before said in the first shewing; where that I saw the Devil is reproved of God, and endless by damned. In which sight I understand, that all the creatures that be of the devils condition in this life and therein ending; there is no more mention made of them before God and all his holy ones, then of the devil; notwithstanding that they be of mankind; whether they have be-christened or not. For though the revelation was shewed of goodness, in which was made litle mention of evil: yet I was not drawn thereby from any point of the faith that Holy Church teacheth me to believe. For I had sight of the passion of Christ in divers shewing; in the *first*, in the *second*, in the *fourth*, in the *eighth*, as it is before said; wherein I had in part feeling of the sorrow of our Lady, and of his true friends that saw his pains: but I saw not so properly specified the Jews that did him to death; but notwithstanding I knew in my faith, that they were accursed and damned without end, saving those that were converted by grace.

And I was strengthed, and learned generally to keep me in the faith, in every point, and in all as I had before understood, hoping that I was therein with mercy and the grace of God, desiring and praying in my meaning, that I might continue therein unto my lives end. It is Gods will that we have great regard to all the deeds that he hath done; for he will thereby that we know, trust and believe all that he shall doe. But evermore us needeth leave the beholding what the deed shall be; and desire we to be like to our brethren which be the saints in heaven, that will right nought but Gods will. Then shall we only enjoy in God, and be well apaid both with hiding and shewing. For I saw verily in our Lords meaning, the more we busie us to know his privities in that or in any other thing, the farther more shall we be from the knowing.

The Thirty-fourth Chapter.

Our Lord shewed two manner of privities. *One* is this great privity, with all the privy points thereto belonging: and these privities he will we know thus hid, into the time that he will clearly shew them to us. *That other* are the privities which himself shewed openly in this revelation; for those are privities which he will make open and known to us: for he will that we wit that it is his will that we know them. They are privities to us, but not only for that he will they be privities to us, but they are privities to us, for our blind-head and our unknowing. And therefore hath he great ruth; and therefore he will make them open to us himself, whereby we may know him, and love him, and cleave to him. For all that is speedeful for us to wit, and for to know, full courteously our good Lord will shew us what it is with all the preaching and teaching of Holy Church, God shewed full great pleasaunce that he hath in all men and women, that mightily and wisely take the preaching and teaching of Holy Church; for he it is Holy Church; he is the ground, he is the substance, he is the teaching, he is the teacher, he is the end, and he is the meed: wherefore every kind soul traveleth. And this is known, and shall be known to each soul to which the Holy Ghost declareth it. And I hope truly all those that seek thus, they shall speed, for they seek God. All this that I have now said, and more as I shall say hereafter, is comforting against sin. For in the *third* shewing, when I saw that God doth all that is done, I saw not sin, and then I saw that all is well; but when God shewed me for sin, then said he, '*All shall be well.*'

The Thirty-fifth Chapter.

AND when God Almighty had shewed so plenteously, and so fully of his goodness, I desired, to wit, of a certain creature that I loved, if it should continue in good living; which I hoped by the grace of God was begun. And in this singular desire it seemed that I letted myself; for I was not taught in this time. And then was I answered in my reason, as it were by a friendful mean; '*Take it generally, and behold the courtesie of thy Lord God, as he shewed to thee; for it is more worship to God to behold him in all, than in any special thing.*' I assented, and therewith I learned, that it is more worship to God to know all thing in general, than to like in any thing in special, and if I should do wisely after this teaching. I hold not be glad for any thing in special, ne greatly diseased for any manner thing, for '*all shall be well.*' For the full-head of joy, is to behold God in all; for by the same blessed might, wisdom, and love, that he made all thing; to the same end, our good Lord leadeth it continually, and there to himself shall bring it, and when it is time we shall see it. And the ground of this was shewed in the *first*, and more openly in the *third*, where it saith; I saw God in a point: All that our Lord doth, is rightfully, and all that he suffereth is worshipful. And in these two is comprehended good and evil; for all that is good our Lord doth, and that is evil our Lord suffereth: I say not that evil is worshipful, but I say the sufferance of our Lord God is worshipful, whereby his goodness shall be known without end, and his marvellous meekness and mild-head by this working of mercy and grace. Right full-head is that thing that is so good, that it may not be better than it is: for God himself is very rightful-head, and all his works be done rightfully, as they be ordained fro without beginning by his high might, his high wisdom, his high goodness. And right, as he hath ordained it to the best, right so he worketh continually, and leadeth it to the same end: And he is ever full pleased with himself, and with all his works. And the beholding of this blessed accord is full sweet to the soul that seeth it by grace. All the souls that shall be saved in heaven without end, be made rightful in the sight of God, and by his own goodness. In which rightfullness we be endlesly kept, and marvellously above all creatures. And mercy is a working that cometh of the goodness of God. And it shall last working as long as sin is suffered to pursue rightful souls: and when sin hath no longer leave to pursue, then shall the working of mercy cease: and then shall all be brought into rightfulness, and therein stand without end. By his sufferance we fall, and in his blessed love with his might, and his wisdom we are kept, and by mercy and grace we be raised to manifold more joy. And thus in rightfulness and in mercy he will be known and loved, now and without end. And the soul that wisely beholdeth in grace is well paid with both, and endlesly enjoyeth.

The Thirty-sixth Chapter.

OUR Lord God shewed that a deed shall be done, and himself shall do it; and it shall be worshipful and marvellous, and plentuous, and by him it shall be done, and himself shall do it. And this is the highest joy that the soul understood, that God himself shall do it. And I shall do right nought but sin, and my sin shall not let his goodness working. And I saw that the beholding of this is a heavenly joy in a dreadful soul, which evermore kindly by grace desireth Gods will. This deed shall be begun here, and it shall be worshipful to God, and plentuously profitable to all his lovers in earth. And ever as we come to heaven, we shall see it in marvellous joy. And it shall last thus in working to the last day; and the worship and the bliss of that shall last in heaven before God, and all his holy saints without end. Thus was this deed seen and understand in our Lords meaning; and the cause why he shewed it, is to make us to enjoy in him and in all his works.

When I saw the shewing continued, I understood it was shewed for a great thing that was then for to come: which thing God shewed that himself should do it. Which deed hath the properties before said. And this shewed he full blessedfully, meaning that I should take it wistly, faithfully, and trustfully; but what the deed should be it was kept privy to me. And in this I saw, he will not we dread to know the things that he sheweth; he sheweth them, for he will we know them. By which knowing, he will we love him, and like in him, and endlesly enjoy in him. And for the great love that he hath to us, he sheweth us all that is worshipful and profitable for the time. And those things that he will now have privy; yet of his great goodness he shewed them close. In which shewing he will we believe, and understand, that we should see it verily in his endless bliss. Then ought we to enjoy in him for all that he sheweth, and all that he hideth. And if we wilfully and meekly do this, we shall find therein great ease, and endless thanking we shall have of him therefore. And this is the understanding of this word, '*That it shall be done by me,*' that is to say, the general man; that is to say, all that shall be safe, it shall be worshipful, marvellous, and plentuous, and '*By me it shall be done, and God himself shall do it.*' And this shall be highest joy that may be beholden of the deed that God himself shall do it, and man shall do right nought but sin. Then meaneth our Lord God thus, as if he said, '*Behold and see, here hast thou matter of meekness; here hast thou matter of love; here hast thou matter of knowing thy self; here hast thou matter of enjoying in me; and for my love enjoy in me, for of all thing, therewith might thou most please mee.*' And as long as we be in this life, what time that we by our folly turn us to the beholding of the reproved, tenderly our Lord toucheth us, and blissedfully calleth us, saying in our soul, '*Let me alone my dear worthy child; intend to me, I am enough to thee, and enjoy in thy Saviour and in thy salvation.*' And that this is our Lords working in us: I am sure the soul that is pearced therewith by grace, shall see it and feel it; and though it be so that this deed be truly take for the general man, yet it excludeth not the special; for what our good Lord will do by his poor creatures, it is now unknown to me. But this deed, and that other aforesaid, it is not both one, but two sundry; but this deed shall be known sooner, and that shall be as we come to heaven. And to whom our Lord giveth it, it may be known here in party. But the great deed aforesaid shall neither be known in heaven nor in earth till that it be done. And furthermore, he gave special understanding and teaching of working, and shewing of miracles as this; '*It is known that I have done miracles here before many, and full high and marvellous, worshipful and great, and so as I have done, I do now continually, and shall in coming of time. It is known that before miracles come, sorrows, and anguish, and trouble.*' And that is, that we should know our own feebleness and mischief that we be fallen in by sin, to meek us, and make us to cry to God for help and grace; and great miracles come after, and that of the high might and wisdom, and goodness of God, shewing his vertue and the joyes of heaven, so as it may be, in this passing life, and that for the strengthening of our faith, and encrease of our hope in charity. Wherefore it pleaseth him to be known and worshipped in miracles. Then meaneth he thus, he will that we be not born over low for sorrows and tempests that fall to us, for it hath ever so been before miracles comming.

The Thirty-seventh Chapter.

GOD brought to mind that I should sin: and for liking that I had in beholding of him, I entented not redily to that shewing. And our Lord full mercifully abode, and gave me grace for to entend. And this shewing I took singularly to myself: but by all the gracious comforts that followeth as ye shall see, I was learned to take it to all mine even Christen, all in general, and nothing in special: though our Lord shewed me that I should sin, by me alone is understood all. And in this I conceived a soft dread: and to this our Lord answered, '*I keep thee full surely.*' This word was said with more love and sureness of ghostly keeping, than I can or may tell: for as it was afore shewed to me that I should sin, right so was the comfort shewed sureness of keeping for all mine even Christen *(Who shall be saved)*. What may make me more to love mine even Christen, than to see in God that he loveth all that shall be saved, as it were all one soul; for in every soul that shall be saved, is a godly will that never finally assenteth to sinn, ne never shall. Right as there is a beastly will in the lower party that may will no good; right so there is a godly will in the higher party; which will is so good, that it may never will evil endlesly, but ever good; and therefore we be that he loveth, and endlesly we do that he liketh. And this shewed our good Lord in the wholehead of love that we stand in his sight, yea that he loveth us now as well while that we be here, as he shall do when we be there before his blessed face. But for failing of love in our party, therefore is all our travel.

The Thirty-eighth Chapter.

AND God shewed that sin shall be no shame but worship to man; for right as to every sin is answering a pain by truth: right so for every sin to the same soul is given a bliss by love. Right as divers sins be punished with divers pains after that it be grievous; right so shall they be rewarded with diverse joys in heaven for their victories, after as the sin hath been painful and sorrowful to the soul in earth; for the soul that shall come to heaven is so precious to God, and the place so worshipful, that the goodness of God suffereth never that soul to sin finally that shall come thither: but what sinners they are that so shall be rewarded, is made known in Holy Church in earth, and also in heaven, by overpassing worships: for in this sight my understanding was lifted up into heaven. And then God brought merily to my mind David, and other in the Old Law with him without number. And in the New Law he brought to my mind, first Magdalen, Peter, and Paul, Thomas, and Jude, St. John of Beverley, and others also without number; how they be known in the church on earth with their sins; and it is to them no shame, but all is turned them to worship. And therefore our courteous Lord sheweth for them here in party, like as it is there fulfilled; for there the token of sin is turned to worship. And St. John of Beverley our Lord shewed him full highly in comfort of us for homeliness (and countrey sake:) and brought to my mind how he is a kind neighbour, and of our knowing: and God called him plainly St. John of Beverley, as we do, and that with a full glad and sweet chear, shewing that he is a full high saint in his sight, and a blessedful: and with this he made mention, that in his youth, and in his tender age, he was a dear worthy servant to God; full greatly God loving and dreading. And nevertheless God suffered him to fall; him mercifully keeping that he perished not, ne lost no time. And afterward God raised him to manifold more grace; and by the contrition and the meekness that he had in his living, God hath given him in heaven manifold joys, overpassing that he should have had, if he had not sinned or fallen. And that this is true, God sheweth in earth with plentuous miracles doing about his body continually. And all this was to make us glad and merry in love.

The Thirty-ninth Chapter.

SIN is the sharpest scourge that any chosen soul may be smitten with. Which scourge all to beateth man or woman, and all to breaketh him, and purgeth him in his own sight: so far forth, that otherwhile he thinketh himself that he is not worthy, but as it were, to sink into hell, till when contrition taketh him by touching of the Holy Ghost, and turneth the bitterness into hope of Gods mercy. And then begin his wounds, to heal, and the soul to quicken, turned into the life of Holy Church. The Holy Ghost leadeth him to confession, wilfully to shew his sins nakedly and truly with great sorrow, and with great shame, that he hath so defouled the fair image of God. Then undertaketh he penance for every sin enjoyned by his domes-man, that is grounded in Holy Church, by the teaching of the Holy Ghost.

And this is one meekness that greatly pleaseth God, and also meekly taketh bodily sickness of God's sending: also sorrow and shame outwardly, with reproof and despite of the world; with all manner of grievance and temptations that we be cast in, ghostly and bodily: full preciously our good Lord keepeth us, when it seemeth to us that we be near forsaken, and cast away for our sin, and for we see that we have deserved it. And because of the meekness that we get thereby, we be raised full high in God's sight by his grace. And also whom our Lord will, he visiteth of his special grace with so great contrition, and also with compassion, and true longing to God, that they be suddenly delivered of sin and of pain, and taken up to bliss, and made even with saints. By contrition, we be made clean;

by compassion, we be made ready; and by true longing to God we be made worthy.

These be *three* means as I understood, whereby that all souls come to heaven; that is to say, that have been sinners in earth, and shall be saved: for by these medicines behoveth that every sinful soul be healed; though that he be healed, his wounds be seen before God not as wounds, but as worships. And so on the contrariwise, as we be punished here with sorrow and with penance, we shall be rewarded in heaven by the courteous love of our God Almighty, that will that none that come there leese his travel in any degree: for he beholdeth sin as sorrow and pains to his lovers, in whom he assigneth no blame for love. The meed that we undertake, shall not be litle, but it shall be high, glorious and worshipful; and so shall all shame turn to worship and to joy. For our courteous Lord will not that his servants despair for oft failing, ne for grievous falling; for our falling letteth not him to love us; peace and love is ever in us, being and working; but we be not ever in peace and in love: but he will we take heed thus, that he is ground of all our whole life in love. And furthermore, that he is our everlasting Keeper, and mightily defendeth us against all our enemies that be full fell, and full fierce upon us. And so much our need is the more; for we give them occasion by our falling.

The Fortieth Chapter.

AND this is a sovereign friendship of our courteous Lord, that he keepeth us so tenderly whiles we be in our sin: and furthermore, he toucheth us full privily, and sheweth us our sin by the sweet light of mercy and grace. But when we see ourself so foul, then we wene that God were wrath with us for our sin. Then be we stirred of the Holy Ghost by contrition into prayer and desire, amending of our self with all our might, to slack the wrath of God, unto the time we find a rest in soul and softness in conscience. And then hope we that God hath forgiven us our sin, and it is true. And then sheweth our courteous Lord himself to the soul merrily, and of full glad chear, with friendfully welcoming as if it had been in pain and in prison, saying thus: '*My dear darling, I am glad thou art come to me in all thy woe; I have ever been with thee, and now seest thou me loving, and we be oned in bliss.*' Thus are sins forgiven by grace and mercy, and our soul worshipfully received in joy; like as it shall be when it cometh into heaven, as oftimes as it cometh by the gracious working of the Holy Ghost, and the vertue of Christs passion. Here understood I verily, that all manner of thing is made ready to us by the great goodness of God; so far forth, that what time we be our self in peace and in charity, we be verily safe. But for we may not have this in fullhead while we be here; therefore it befalleth us ever to live in sweet praying, and in lovely longing with our Lord Jesu, for he longeth ever for to bring us to the fulhead of joy, as it is before said; where he sheweth the ghostly thirst.

But now because of all this ghostly comfort that is before said; if any man or woman be stirred by folly, to say or to think; "If this be true, then were it good for to sin, to have the more meed, or else to charge the less to sin." Beware of this stirring, for truly if it come, it is untrue, and of the enemy: for the same true love that toucheth us all by his blessed comfort; the same blessed love teacheth us that we shall hate sin only for love. And I am sure by my own feeling, the more that each kind soul seeth this in the courteous love of our Lord God, the lother is him to sin, and the more he is ashamed: for if it were laid before us all the pain that is in hell, and in purgatory, and in earth, to suffer it rather than sin, we should rather choose all that pain, than sin: for sin is so vile, and so mickle for to hate, that it may be likned to no pain; which pain is not sin. And to me was shewed none harder hell than sin; for a kind soul hateth no pain but sin, for all is good but sin, and naught is evil but sin. And when we give our intent to love and meekness, by the working of mercy and grace, we be made all fair and clean.

And as mighty, and as wise as God is to save man, as willing he is. For Christ himself is ground of all the laws of Christen men; and he taught us to doe good against evil. Here we may see that he is himself this charity, and doth to us as he teacheth us to do: for he will that we be like him in whole-head of endless love to our self, and to our even Christen. No more than his love is broken to us for our sin, no more will he that our love be broken to our self, nor to our even Christen, but nakedly hate sin, and endlesly love the soul, as God loveth it. Then should we hate sin like as God hateth it, and love the soul as God loveth it; for these words that God said, is an endless comfort, '*I keep thee full truly.*'

The Fourteenth Revelation.

The Forty-first Chapter.

After this our Lord shewed for prayer: in which shewing, I saw two conditions in our Lords meaning. *One* is rightful prayer. *Another* is siker trust. But yet oftentimes our trust is not full; for we be not sure that God heareth us, as we think for our unworthiness, and for we feel right naught; for we be as barren, and as dry ofttimes after our prayers as we were before. And thus in our feelling, our folly is cause of our weakness: for thus have I felt by my self. And all this brought our Lord suddenly to my mind, and shewed these words, and said, '*I am ground of thy beseeking. First, it is my will that thou have it: and sithen I make thee to will it: and sithen I make thee to beseek it, and thou seekest it: How should it then be, that thou shouldest not have thy seeking?*' And thus in the first reason, with the three that follow, our good Lord sheweth a mighty comfort, as it may be seen in the same words; and in the first reason, there he saith; '*And thou beseek it:*' there he sheweth full great pleasance and endless meed, that he will give us for our beseeking. And in the sixth reason, there he saith, '*How should it then be?*' This was said for an unpossible thing; for it is the most unpossible that may, that we should seek mercy and grace, and not have it. For of all thing that our good Lord maketh us to beseek himself, he hath ordained it to us from without beginning. Here may we then see, that our beseeking is not the cause of the goodness and grace that he doth to us, but his proper goodness. And that shewed he verily in all these sweet words, there he saith, '*I am ground.*' And our good Lord will that this be known of his lovers in earth; and the more that we know, the more shall we beseech, if it be wisely take; and so is our Lords meaning. Beseeching is a true and gracious lasting will of the soul, owned and fastened into the will of our Lord, by the sweet privy working of the Holy Ghost. Our Lord himself he is the first receiver of our prayer, as to my sight, and he taketh it full thankfully; and highly enjoying, he sendeth it up above, and setteth it in treasure, where it shall never perish: it is there before God, with all his holy saints continually received, ever speeding our needs. And when we shall undertake our bliss, it shall be given us for a degree of joy, with endless worshipful thanking of him; full glad and merry is our Lord of our prayer: and he looketh thereafter, and he will have it; for with his grace it maketh us like to himself in condition, as we be in kind; and so is his blessed will: for he saith thus, '*Pray intirely, inwardly, though thee think it savour thee not, yet it is profitable enough, though thou feel it nought: pray intirely, inwardly, though thou feel nought, though thou see nought; yea, though thou think thou might not; for in dryness, and barrenness, in sickness, and in feebleness, then is thy prayer full pleasant to mee; though thou think it savor thee not but litle, and so is all thy living prayer in my sight.*'

For the meed and the endless thank that he will give us, therefore he is covetuous to have us praying continually in his sight. God accepteth the good will, and the travel of his servants, howsoever we feel: wherefore it pleaseth him that we work in prayer, and in good living, by his help and his grace, reasonably with discretion, keeping our mights to him; till when we have him that we seek in fulhead of joy, that is Jesu. And that shewed he in the xvth Revelation, where he saith, '*Thou shalt have me to thy meed.*' Also to prayer longeth thanking: thanking is a true inward knowing, with great reverence and lovely dreed, turning our self with all our mights into the working that our Lord stirred us to enjoying and thanking inwardly: and sometime for plentuousness it breaketh out with voyce, and saith, 'Good Lord, grant mercy; blessed mote thou be.' And sometime when the earth is dry, and feeleth naught; or else by temptation of our enemy, then it is driven by reason and by grace to cry upon our Lord with voyce, rehearsing his blessed passion, and his great goodness. And so the vertue of our Lords word turneth into the soul, and quickeneth the heart, and entreth by his grace into true working, and maketh it to pray full blessedfully, and truly to enjoy in our Lord, is a full lovely thanking in his sight.

The Forty-second Chapter.

OUR Lord will that we have true understanding, and namely in *three* things that longeth to our prayer: the *first* is, by whom and how that our prayer springeth; by whom, he sheweth when he saith, '*I am ground;*' and how by his goodness: for he saith, '*First it is my will.*'

For the *second*, in what manner, and how that we should use our prayers; and that is, that our will be turned into the will of our Lord enjoying: and so he meaneth when he saith, '*I make thee to will it.*' For the *third*, that we know the fruit and end of our prayer; that is to be oned, and like to our Lord in all thing; and to this meaning, and for this end, was all this lovely lesson shewed: and he will help us, and he shall make it so as he seeth himself; blessed mote he be: for this is our Lords will that our prayer and our trust he both alike large; for if we trust not as mickle as we pray, we do not full worship to our Lord in our prayer. And also we tarry and pain our self; and the cause is as I believe, for we know not truly that our Lord is ground in whom that our prayer springeth. And also that we know not that it is given us by grace of his love; for if we knew this, it would make us to trust to have of our Lords gift all that we desire; for I am sure that no man asketh mercy and grace with true meaning, but if mercy and grace be first given to him. But sometime it cometh to our mind that we have prayed long time; and yet it thinketh us that we have not our asking: but herefore should we not be heavy; for I am sure by our Lords meaning, that either we abide a better time, or more grace, or a better gift. He will that we have true knowing in himself that he is being. And in this knowing, he will that our understanding be grounded with all our mights, and all our intents, and all our meanings: and in this ground, he will that we take our steeds, and our dwelling. And by the gracious light of himself, he will that we have understanding of *three* things that follow. The *first* is, our noble and excellent making. The *second*, our precious and dear worthy again being. The *third*, all thing that he hath made beneath us, to serve us, and for our love keepeth it. Then meaneth he thus, as if he said, '*Behold and see that I have done all this before thy prayer, and now thou art, and prayest me.*' And thus he meaneth that it longeth to us, to wit, that the greatest deeds be done, as Holy Church teacheth. And in the beholding of this, with thanking, we owe to pray for the deed that is now in doing; and that is, that he rule us, and guide us to his worship in this life, and bring us to his bliss; and therefore he hath done all. Then meaneth he thus, that we see that he doth it; and we pray therefore, for that one is not enough: for if we pray, and see not that he doth it, it maketh us heavy and doubtful, and that is not his worship. And if we see that doth it, and we pray not, we do not our duty: and so it may not be; that is to say, so is it not in his beholding. But to see that he doth it, and to pray forthwithall: so is he worshipped, and we speed. All thing that our Lord hath ordained to doe, it is his will that we pray therefore, either in special or in general. And the joy and the bliss that is to him, and the thank and the worship that we shall have therefore, it passeth the understanding of all creatures in this life, as to my sight. For prayer is a rightwise understanding of that fullhead of joy that is for to come, with true longing, and very trust savouring or seeing our bliss, that we be ordained to, kindly maketh us to long. True understanding and love, with sweet meaning in our Saviour graciously maketh us to trust. And thus have we of kind to long, and of grace to trust: and in these two workings, our Lord beholdeth us continually; for it is our duty. And his goodness may no less assigne in us, that longeth to us, to doe our diligence thereto: and when we do it, yet shall us think that it is naught: and true it is, but doe we as we may, and meekly ask mercy and grace; and all that us faileth, we shall it find in him. And thus meaneth he, there he saith, '*I am the ground of thy beseeching.*' And thus in those blessedful words, with the shewing, I saw a full overcoming against all our wickedness, and all our doubtful dreeds.

The Forty-third Chapter.

PRAYER owneth the soul to God, which is ever like to God in kind and in substance, restored by grace; but it is oft unlike in condition, by sin of mans party. Then is prayer a witness that the soul will as God will; and comforteth the conscience, and ableth man to grace. And thus he teacheth us to pray; and mightily to trust that we shall have it; for he beholdeth us in love, and will make us partner of his good will and deed: and therefore he stirreth us to pray, that that liketh him to do: for which prayer and good will that we have of his gift, he will reward us, and give us endless meed. And this was shewed in this word, '*And thou beseekest it.*' In this word God shewed so great pleasance, and so great liking, as he were much beholding to us for each good deed that we do; and yet it is he that doth it: and for that we beseech him mightily, to do that thing that him liketh; as if he said, '*What might thou please mee more than to beseech mightily, wisely, and wilfully, to do that thing that I will have done.*' And thus the soul by prayer is accorded with God. But when our courteous Lord of his special grace sheweth himself to our soul, we have that we desire: and then we see not for the time what we should more pray; but all our intent, with all our mights is set whole into the beholding of him. And this is an high unperceiveable prayer, as to my sight; for all the cause wherefore we prayer, is to be oned in to the sight and beholding of him, to whom we pray marvellously, enjoying with reverent dreed; and so great sweetness, and delight in him, that we can pray right naught, but as he stirreth us for the time. And well I wot, the more the soul seeth of God, the more she desireth him by grace; but when we see him not so, then feel we need, and cause to pray for feeling, and for unableness of our self to Jesu.

For when a soul is tempted, troubled, and left to herself by her unrest, then it is time to pray to make her self supple and buxom to God; but she by no manner of prayer maketh God supple to him, for he is ever one like in love.

And thus I saw, that what time we see need, wherefore we pray; then our Lord God followeth us, helping our desire: and when we of his special grace plainly behold him, seeing none of other needs, then we follow him. And he draweth us to him by love, for I saw, and felt that his marvellous, and his fulsome goodness fulfilleth all our mights. And therewith I saw that his continual working in all manner of things, is done so godly, so wisely, and so mightily, that it over-passeth all our imagining, and all that we can mean or think. And then we can do no more but behold him, and enjoy with a high mighty desire to be all oned into him, and entend to his motion, and enjoy in his loving, and delight in his goodness. And thus shall we with his sweet grace in our own meek continual prayer, come into him; now in this life, by many privy touchings of sweet ghostly sights and feelings, measured to us as our simplehead may bare it. And this is wrought, and shall be by the grace of the Holy Ghost, so long till we shall die in longing for love; and then shall we all come into our Lord, our self clearly knowing, and God fulsomely having: and we endlesly be all hid in God, verily seeing, and fulsomely feeling him ghostly hearing; and him delectably smelling, and him sweetly smelling: and there shall we see God face to face homely, and fulsomely. The creature which is made, shall see, and endlesly behold God which is the Maker; for thus may no man see God and live after; that is to say, in this deadly life: but when he of his special grace will shew him here, he strengtheneth the creature above himself, and he measureth the shewing after his own will, and it is profitable for the time.

The Forty-fourth Chapter.

God shewed in all the Revelations ofttimes that (a holy) man worketh evermore his will and his worship, duringly without stinting: and what this working is, was shewed in the *first*, and that in a marvellous ground: for it was shewed in the working of the blissedful soul of our Lady Saint Mary by truth and wisdom. And how, I hope by the grace of the Holy Ghost, I shall say as I saw. Truth seeth God, and wisdom beholdeth God; and of these two, cometh the third; and that is, a marvellous delight in God which is love: where truth and wisdom is verily, there is love verily coming of them both, and all of Gods making: for God is endless soveraign truth, endless soveraign wisdom, endless soveraign love unmade. And a mans soul is a creature in God, which hath the same properties made; and evermore it doth that it was made for; that seeth God, it beholdeth God, and it loveth God: wherefore God enjoyeth in the creature, and the creature in God endlesly marvelling. In which marvelling he seeth his God, his Lord, his Maker so high, so great, and so good, in regard of him that is made, that unneth the creature seemeth ought to the self; but the brightness and clearness of truth and wisdom maketh him to see, and to know, that he is made for love; in which love God endlesly keepeth him.

The Forty-fifth Chapter.

God deemeth us upon our kindly substance, which is ever kept one in him, whole and safe without end. And this doome is of his rightful-head: and man deemeth upon our changeable sensuality, which seemeth now one, now another, after that it taketh of the parties, and shewed outward. And this doome is meddled; for sometimes it is good and easie; and sometime it is hard and grievous: and in as much as it is good and easie, it longeth to the rightfulness; and in as much as it is hard and grievous, our good Lord Jesu reformeth it by mercy and grace, through vertue of his blessed passion, and so bringeth into the rightfulness. And though these two be thus accorded and oned, yet it shall be known both in heaven, without end. The first doome which is of Gods rightfulness, and that is of his own high endless love; and that is that fair sweet doome that was shewed in all the fair revelation; in which I saw him assigne to us no manner of blame. And though these were sweet and delectable, yet only in the beholding of this, I could not be full eased: and that was for the doome of Holy Church, which I had before understanding, and was continually in my sight. And therefore by this doome, me thought that me behooveth needs to know my self a sinner: and by the same doome I understood, that sinners be sometimes worthy blame and wrath; and these two could I not see in God: and therefore my advise and desire was more than I can or may tell; for the higher doome God sheweth himself in the same time. And therefore me behooved needs to take it: and the lower doome was learned me before time in Holy Church; and therefore I might not by no way leave the lower doome. Then was this my desire, that I might see in God, in what manner that the doome of Holy Church here in earth, is true in his sight, and how it longeth to me verily to know it, whereby they might both be saved, so as it were worshipful to God, and right way to me. And to all this, I ne had no other answer, but a marvellous example of a lord, and of a servant, as I shall say after, and that full mistely shewed: and yet I stood in desire, and will, into my lives end, that I might by grace know these two dooms, as it longeth to me. For all heavenly things, and all earthly things that long to heaven, be comprehended in these two dooms. And the more knowing, and understanding, by the gracious leading of the Holy Ghost, that we have of these two dooms; the more we shall see and know our feelings *(and workings of grace);* and ever the more that we see them, the more kindly by grace, we shall long to be fulfilled of endless joy and bliss, for we be made thereto. And our kindly substance is now blessedfully in God, and hath been sithens it was made, and shall be without end.

The Forty-sixth Chapter.

BUT our passing living that we have here in our sensuality, knoweth not what our self is, but in our faith. And when we know, and see verily, and clearly what our self is, then shall we verily and clearly see, and know our Lord God in fulhead of joy. And therefore it behoveth needs to be, that the nearer we be our bliss, the more we shall long; and that both by kind and by grace: we may have knowing of our self in this life, by continual help and vertue of our high kind; in which knowing, we may encrease and wax by furthering and speeding of mercy and grace. But we may never full know our self into the last point: in which point, this passing life, and all manner of woe and paine shall have an end. And therefore it longeth properly to us both by grace and by kind, to long and desire, with all our mights to know our self. In which full knowing, we shall verily and clearly know our God in fulhead of endless joy. And yet in all this time fro the beginning to the end, I had *two* manner of beholdings: the *one* was endless continuant love; with sureness of keeping, and blissful salvation, for of this was all the shewing. That *other*, was the common teaching of Holy Church, of which I was before enformed and grounded, and wilfully having in use, and understanding. And the beholding of this came not from me; for by the shewing, I was not stirred, nor led therefro in no manner point. But I had therein teaching to love it, and like it; whereby I might with the help of our Lord and his grace, increase and rise to more heavenly knowing, and higher loving. And thus in all this beholding, methought it behoved needs to see and to know that we be sinners, and do many evils that we ought to leave, and leave many good deeds undone that we ought to do: wherefore we deserve pain, blame, and wrath. And notwithstanding all this, I saw verily that our Lord was never wrath, ne never shall: for he is God, he is good, he is truth, he is love, and he is peace; and his might, his wisdom, his charity, and his unity suffereth him not to be wrath: for I saw truly that it is against the property of his might to be wrath; and against the property of his wisdom, and against the property of his goodness. God is that goodness that may not be wrath, for God is not but goodness. Our soul is oned to him, unchangeable goodness: and between God and our soul is neither wrath nor forgiveness in his sight; for our soul is so fulsomely oned to God of his own goodness, that between God and our soul may be right naught. And to this understanding was the soul led by love, and drawn by might in every shewing: that it is thus, our good Lord shewed; and how it is thus verily of his great goodness, and that he will we desire, to wit; that is to say, as it longeth to his creatures to wit it for all thing that the simple soul understood, God will that it be shewed and known for those things that he will have privy, mightily and wisely himself hideth them for love; for I saw in the same shewing, that much privity is hid, which may never be known into the time that God of his goodness hath made us worthy to see it. And therewith I am well apaid, abiding our Lords will in this high marvel. And now I yield me to our mother Holy Church, as a simple child oweth.

The Forty-seventh Chapter.

Two points belonging to our soul are debt. *One* is, that we reverently marvel. That *other* is, that we meekly suffer, every enjoying in God; for he will that we know, that we shall in short time see clearly in himself all that we desire. And notwithstanding all this, I beheld and marvelled greatly, what is the mercy and forgiveness of God? For by the teaching that I had before, I understood that the mercy of God shall be forgiveness of his wrath, after the time that we have sinned: for methought that to a soul whose meaning and desire is to love, that the wrath of God were harder than any other pain. And therefore I took, that the forgiveness of his wrath should be one of the principal points of his mercy. But for ought that I might behold and desire, I could not see this point in all the shewing. But how I saw and understood of the working of mercy; I shall say some deal, as God will give me grace. I understood thus; man is changeable in this life, and by simpleness and uncunning falleth into sin: he is unmighty, and unwise of himself; and also his will is over-laid. In this time he is in tempest, and in sorrow, and in woe: and the cause is blindness, for he seeth not God; for if he saw God continually, he should have no mischievous feeling, ne no manner stirring, nor sorrowing that serveth to sin. Thus saw I, and felt in the same time; and methought that the sight and the feeling was high, and plentuous, and gracious, in regard that our common feeling is in this life; but yet methought it was but low and small, in regard of the great desire that the soul hath to see God: for I felt in me *five* manner of workings, which be these; enjoying, mourning, desire, dreed, and true hope. Enjoying for God, gave me understanding, and knowing that it was himself that I saw mourning, and that was for feeling desire, that was that I might see him for ever more and more; understanding and knowing, that we shall never have full rest, till we see him clearly and verily in heaven. Dreed was, for it seemed to me in all that time, that sight should fail, and I to be left to myself. True hope, was in the endless love that I saw, that I should be kept by his mercy, and brought to the bliss. And the joying in his sight, with this true hope of his merciful keeping, made me to have feeling and comfort: so that mourning and dreed were not greatly painful. And yet in all this, I beheld in the shewing of God, that this manner sight of him may not be continuant in this life; and that for his own worship, and for increase of our endless joy. And therefore we fail oftentimes of the sight of him: and anon we fall into our self, and then find we feeling of right naught but the contrarious that is in our self. And that of the old root of our first sin, with all that followeth of our own continuance: and in this we be travelled and tempted, with feeling of sin and of pain in many diverse manner, ghostly and bodily, as it is known to us in this life.

The Forty-eighth Chapter.

But our good Lord the Holy Ghost, which is endless life dwelling in our soul, full truly keepeth us, and worketh therein a peace, and bringeth it to ease by grace, and maketh it buxom, and accordeth it to God. And this is the mercy and the way that our good Lord continually leadeth us in, as long as we be in this life, which is changeable: for I saw no wrath but on mans party, and that forgiveth he in us: for wrath is not else but a frowardness, and a contrariousness to peace and love. And either it cometh of feeling of might, or of feeling of wisdom, or of feeling of goodness: which feeling is not of God, but it is in our party; for we by sin and wretchedness have in us a wrath, and a continuant contrariousness to peace and to love. And that shewed he full oft in his lovely chear of ruth and pity: for the ground of mercy is in love, and the working of mercy is our keeping in love: and this was shewed in such a manner, that I could not perceive of the property of mercy otherwise, but as it were all love in love; that is to say, as to my sight, mercy is a sweet gracious working in love, medled with plenteous pitty; for mercy worketh, us keeping; and mercy worketh turning to us all thing to good: mercy for love suffereth us to fail by measure, and in as much as we fail, in so much we fall; and in as much as we fall, in so much we die: for us behooveth needs to die, in as much as we fail sight and feeling of God, that is our life. Our failing is dreadful, our falling is shameful; and our dying is sorrowful. But yet in all this the sweet eye of pity and love departeth never from us, ne the working of mercy ceaseth not: for I beheld the property of mercy, and I beheld the property of grace, which have *two* manner of working in one love: mercy is a pitiful property, which longeth to mother-hood in tender love: and grace is a worshipful property which longeth to royal lordship in the same love. Mercy worketh, keeping, suffering, quickening, and healing, and all is of tenderness of love: and grace worketh with mercy, raising, rewarding, endlesly over-passing, that our loving, and our travel deserveth, spreading abroad, and shewing the high plenteousness, largeness of Gods royal lordship in his marvellous courtesie. And this is of the abundance of love; for grace worketh our dreadful failing into plenteous and endless solace: and grace worketh our shameful falling into high worshipful rising; and grace worketh our sorrowful dying into holy blissful life: for I saw full truly that ever as our contrariousness worketh to us here in earth, pain, shame, and sorrow. Right so on the contrariwise, grace worketh to us in heaven, solace, worship, and bliss; and over-passing so far forth, that when we come up and receive that sweet reward which grace hath wrought to us there, we shall thank and bless our Lord endlesly, enjoying that ever we suffered woe; and that shall be for a property of blessed love that we shall know in God, which we might never have known without woe going before. And when I saw all this, me behooved needs to grant that the mercy of God and the forgiveness slacketh and wasteth our wrath.

The Forty-ninth Chapter.

FOR it was an high marvel to the soul which was continuantly shewed in all, and with great diligence, beholding that our Lord God aneynst himself may not forgive, for he may not be wrath. It were unpossible; for this was shewed, that our life is all grounded and rooted in love, and without love we may not live. And therefore to the soul, that of his special grace, seeth so far forth of the high marvellous goodness of God, that we be endlesly oned to him in love: it is the most unpossible that may be, that God should be wrath; for wrath and friendship be *two* contraries; for he that wasteth and destroyeth our wrath, and maketh us meek and mild; it behooveth us needs to believe, that he be ever in one love, meek, and mild: which is contrary to wrath, for I saw full truly, that where our Lord appeareth, peace is taken, and wrath hath no steede: for I saw no manner of wrath in God, neither for short time, nor for long; for truly as so my sight, if God might be wrath a while, we should neither have life, ne steede, ne being; for as verily as we have our being of the endless might of God, and of the endless wisdom, and of the endless goodness: also verily we have our keeping in the endless might of God, in the endless wisdom, and in the endless goodness. For though we feel in us wrath, debate, and strife, yet we be all mercifully beclosed in the midhead of God, and in his meekhead, in his benignity, and in his buxomness. For I saw full truly, that all our endless friendship, our steed, our life, and our being is in God; for that same endless goodness that keepeth us when we sin, that we perish not: that same endless goodness continually treateth in us a peace against our wrath, and our contrarious falling, and maketh us to see our need, with a true dread mightily to seek unto God to have forgiveness, with a gracious desire of our salvation, for we may not be blissfully saved, till we be verily in peace and in love, for that is our salvation. And though we be wrath, and the contrariousness that is in us be now in tribulation, disease, and woe, as falling into our blindness, and our pronity; yet be we sure and safe by the merciful keeping of God that we perish not; but we be not blissfully safe, in having of our endless joy, till we be all in peace and in love; that is to say, full pleased with God, and with all his works, and with all his dooms; and loving and pleasable with our selves, and with our even Christen, and with all that God loveth, as love liketh. And this doth Gods goodness in us. Thus saw I that God is our very peace; and he is our sure keeper, when we be our self at unpeace; and he continually worketh to bring us into endless peace: and thus when by the working of mercy and grace we be made meek and mild, than we be full safe. Suddenly is the soul oned to God, when she is truly peaced in herself; for in him is found no wrath. And thus I saw when we be all in peace and in love, we find no contrariousness in no manner of letting. And that contrariousness which is now in us, our Lord God of his goodness maketh it to us full profitable: for contrariousness is cause of all our tribulation, and all our woe: and our Lord Jesu taketh them, and sendeth them up to heaven; and then they are made more sweet and delectable than heart may think, or tongue can tell. And when we come thither, we shall find them ready all turned into very fairness and endless worship. Thus is God our stedfast ground, and shall be our full bliss, and make us unchangeable, as he is when we be there.

The Fiftieth Chapter.

AND in this deadly life mercy and forgiveness is our way, that evermore leadeth us to grace. And by the tempest and the sorrow that we fall in on our party, we be often dead as to mans doome in earth; but in the sight of God, the soul that shall be safe, was never dead, ne never shall be. But yet here I wondred and marvelled with all the diligence of my soul meaning thus; 'Good Lord, I see that thou art the very truth, and I know truly that we sin grievously all day, and be much blameworthy: and I may neither leave the knowing of this sooth, nor I see not the shewing to us no manner of blame. How may this be? for I know by the common teaching of Holy Church, and by mine own feeling, that the blame of our sins continually hangeth upon us fro the first man, into the time that we come up into heaven.' Then was this my marvel, that I saw our Lord God shewing to us no more blame, than if we were as clean, and as holy as angels be in heaven. And between these two contraries, my reason was greatly travelled by my blindness, and could have no rest, for dread that his blessed presence should pass from my sight, and I to be left in unknowing how he behold us in our sin; for either me behooved to see in God that sin were all done away, or else me behooved to see in God how he seeth it; whereby I might truly know how it longeth to mee to see sin, and the manner of our blame. My longing endured, him continually beholding; and yet I could have no patience for great fear and perplexity, thinking if I take it thus, that we be no sinners, nor no blame worthy; it seemeth as I should erre, and fail of knowing of this sooth. And if it be true that we be sinners, and blame worthy, good Lord, how may it then be that I cannot see this truth in thee; which art my God, my Maker, in whom I desire to see all truth? For *three* points make me hardy to ask it. The *first* is, for it is so low a thing, for if it were an high, I should be adred. The *second* is, that it is so common; for if it were special and privy also, I should be adred. The *third* is, that it needeth me to wit, as me thinketh; if I shall live here for knowing of good and evil, whereby I may by reason and by grace the more depart them asunder, and love goodness, and hate evil, as Holy Church teacheth. I cried inwardly with all my might, seeking unto God for help; meaning thus, 'Ah Lord Jesu, King of bliss, how shall I be eased?' Who shall tell me, and teach me that me needeth to wit, if I may not at this time see it in thee?

The Fifty-first Chapter.

AND then our courteous Lord answered in shewing full mistely, by a wonderful example of a lord that hath a servant, and gave me sight to my understanding of both: which sight was shewed *double* in the lord; and the sight was shewed *double* in the servant. That *one party* was shewed ghostly in bodily likeness. That *other party* was shewed more ghostly without bodily likeness. For the *first*, thus I saw two persons in bodily likeness; that is to say, a lord and a servant. And therewith God gave me ghostly understanding: the lord sitteth solemnly in rest and in peace; the servant standeth before his lord reverently ready to do his lords will: the lord looketh upon his servant full lovely, and sweetly, and meekly; he sendeth him into a certain place to do his will. The servant not only he goeth, but suddenly he starteth, and runneth in great haste for love to do his lords will. And anon he falleth in a slade, and taketh full great sorrow; and then he groneth, and moneth, and walloweth, and wrieth; but he may not rise nor help himself by no manner of way. And of all this the most mischief that I saw him in, was failing of comfort; for he could not turn his face to look up on his loving lord, which was to him full near, in whom is full comfort: but as a man that was full feeble and unwise for the time he entended to his feeling and enduring in woe. In which woe he suffered *seven* great pains. The *first* was the sore brusing that he took in his falling, which was to him much pain. The *second* was the heaviness of his body. The *third* was feebleness that followed of these two. The *fourth* was, that he was blinded in his reason, and stonnyed in his mind, so far forth, that almost he had forgotten his own love. The *fifth* was, that he might not rise. The *sixth* was pain most marvellous to me; and that was that he lay alone. I looked all about and beheld, and far, ne near, ne high, ne low; I saw to him no help. The *seventh* was, that the place that he lay in, was long, hard, and grievous. I marvelled how this servant might thus meekly suffer all this woe. And I beheld with avisement, to wit, if I could perceive in him any default; or if the lord should assign him any manner of blame. And verily there was none seen; for only his good will and his great desire was the cause of his falling. And he was as unlothful, and as good inwardly as he was when he stood before his lord, ready to do his will. And right thus continually, his loving lord full tenderly beholdeth him; and now with a double chear: *one outward* full meekly and mildly with great rewth and pity; and this was of the *first*. *Another inward* more ghostly: and this was shewed with a leading of my understanding into the Lord in restoring, which I saw him highly enjoy for the worshipful resting, and noble that he will, and shall bring his servant to by his plenteous grace; and this was of *the other* shewing. And now was my understanding led again into the *first*, both keeping in mind: then said this courteous lord in his meaning: '*To my beloved servant, what harm and disease he hath had, and taken in my service for my love, yea, and for his good will? It is not reason that I reward him, his frey and his dreed, his hurt and his maym, and all his woe? and not only this, but falleth it not to me to give him a gift, that be better to him, and more worshipful than his own heal should have been; or else methinketh I did him no grace.'* And in this, an inward ghostly shewing of the lords meaning descended into my soul, in which I saw, that it behooved needs to be standing his great goodness and his own worship, that his dear worthy servant which he loved so much, should be highly and worshipfully rewarded without end, above that he should have been if he had not fallen; yea, and so far forth, that his falling and all his woe that he hath taken thereby, shall be turned into the high over-passing worship and endless bliss: and at this point, the shewing of the example vanished, and our good Lord led forth my understanding, in sight and in shewing of the revelation to the end. But notwithstanding all this forth leading, the marvelling of the example went never from me; for methought it was given me for answer to my desire: and yet could I not take therein full understanding to my ease in that time; for in the servant that was shewed for Adam; as I shall say, I saw many divers properties that might by no manner be direct to single Adam. And thus in that time I stood mickle in *three* knowings; for the full understanding of this marvellous example was not given me in that time. In which misty example, the privities of the revelation be yet much hid. And notwithstanding this, I saw and understood that every shewing is full of privities: and therefore me behooveth now to tell *three* properties, in which I am somedeal eased. The *first* is, the beginning of teaching that I understood there in the same time. The *second* is, the inward learning that I have understood therein sithens. The *third* is, all the holy revelation from the beginning to the end, which our Lord God of his goodness bringeth ofttimes freely to the sight of my understanding. And these *three* be so oned as to my understanding, that I cannot, nor may depart them. And by these *three* as one, I have teaching whereby I owe to believe and trust in our Lord God, that of the same goodness that he shewed it, and for the same end, right so of the same goodness and of the same end; he shall declare it to us when it is his will; for twenty years after the time of the shewing, save three months I had teaching inwardly, as I shall say. It longeth to thee to take heed to all the properties and the conditions that were shewed in the example, though thee think that it be misty and indifferent to thy sight. I assented wilfully with great desire, seeing inwardly with avisement all the points and the properties that were shewed in the same time, as far forth as my wit and my understanding will serve; beginning at my beholding at the lord and at the servant: at the manner of sitting of the lord, and the place he sat on; and the colour of his cloathing; and the manner of shape; and his chear without, and his nobley, and his goodness within: and the manner of standing of the servant; and the place where, and how: and his manner of cloathing, the colour; and the shape at his outward behaviour; and at his inward goodness, and his unlothfulness. The lord, that sat solemnly in rest and in peace, I understand that he is God. The servant that stood before him, I understood that he was shewed for Adam; that is to say, one man was shewed that time, and his falling, to make thereby to be understood how God beholdeth all man and his falling: for in the sight of God, all man is one man, and one man is all man. This man was hurt in his might, and made full feeble: and he was stonnyed in his understanding; for he was turned from the beholding of his lord, but his will was kept in Gods sight: for his will I saw our Lord commend and approve, but himself was letted and blinded of the knowing of this will: and this is to him great sorrow, and grievous disease; for neither he seeth clearly his loving lord, which is to him full meek and mild; nor he seeth truly what himself is in the sight of his loving lord. And well I wot, that when these two be wisely and truly seen, we shall get rest and peace here in party: and the fulsomness in the bliss in heaven by his plentuous grace: and this was a beginning of teaching which I saw in the same time, whereby I might come to knowing, in what manner he beholdeth us in our sin. And then I saw that only pain blameth and punisheth. And our courteous Lord comforteth and succoureth. And ever he is to the soul in glad chear, longing and loving to bring us to his bliss. The place that the lord sat on was simple, on the earth barren and desert, alone in wilderness; his cloathing was wide and side, and full seemly, as falleth to a lord: the colour of the cloathing was blew as azure, most sad and fair; his chear was merciful: the colour of his face was fair, brown, white, with full seemly countenance; his eyen were black, most fair and seemly, shewing full of lovely pity. And within him an heyward long and broad, all full of endless heavenliness: and the lovely looking that he looked on his servant continually; and namely, in his falling; methought it might melt our hearts for love, and burst them in two for joy. This fair looking shewed of a seemly medelur, which was marvellous to behold. That *one* was rewth and pity: that *other* joy and bliss: The joy and bliss passeth as far the ruth and the pity, as heaven is above earth: the pity was earthly, and the bliss heavenly. The rewth and the pity of the Father was of the falling of Adam, which is his most loved creature: the joy and the bliss was of the falling of his dear worthy Son, which is even with the Father. The merciful beholding of his lovely chear, fulfilled all earth, and descended down with Adam into hell; with which continuant pity, Adam was kept fro endless death. And this mercy and pity dwelleth with mankind, into the time that we come up into heaven. But man is blinded in this life, and therefore, we may not see our Father God as he is. And what time that he of his goodness will shew him to man, he sheweth him homely as may, notwithstanding that I saw verily, we ought to know and believe, that the Father is not man. But his sitting on the earth barren and desert, is this to mean: he made mans soul to be his own city, and his dwelling place; which is most pleasing to him of all his works. And what time man was fallen into sorrow and pain; he was not all seemly to serve of that noble office. And therefore our kind Father would have dight him none other place, but to sit upon the earth; abiding mankind, which is medled with earth: till what time by his grace, his dear worthy Son had brought again his city into the noble fairness, with his hard travel. The blewhead of that cloathing betokeneth his stedfastness: the brownhead of his fair face, with the seemly blackhead of the eyen, was most according to shew his holy soberness. The largeness of his cloathing, which was fair flaming about, betokeneth that he hath beclosed in him all heaviness, and all endless joy and bliss. And this was shewed in a touch; where I saw that my understanding was led into the Lord, in which I saw him highly enjoy, for the worshipful restoring, that he will and shall bring his servant to by his plentious grace. And yet I marvelled, beholding the lord and the servant before said: I saw the lord sit solemnly, and the servant standing reverently before his lord: in which servant is *double* understanding; *one* without, an *other* within; outward he was clad simple, as a labourer which was disposed to travel, and he stood full near the lord, not even fore anenst him; but in party aside, and that on the left side. His cloathing was a white kirtle, single, old, and all defaulted, dyed with sweat of his body; streit sitting to him, and short as it were an handful beneath the knee; bare, seeming as it should soon be worn up, ready to be ragged and rent. And in this I marvelled greatly, thinking, this is now an unseemly cloathing for the servant that is so highly loved, to stand in before so worshipful a lord. And inward in him was shewed a ground of love; which love, he had to the lord, that was even like to the love that the lord had to him. The wisdom of the servant saw inwardly, that there was one thing to do, which should be worship to the lord. And the servant for love, having no regard to himself, nor to nothing that might fall off him, hastily did start and run at the sending of his lord, to do that thing which was his will and his worship; for it seemed by his outward cloathing, as if he had been a continuant labourer, and an hard traveller of long time. And by the inward sight that I had, both in the lord and in the servant, it seemed that he was anaved; that is to say, new beginning for to travel; which servant was never sent out before. There was a treasure in the earth which the lord loved; I marvelled and thought what it might be: and I was answered in my understanding, it is a meat which is lovesome and pleasing unto the lord: for I saw the lord sit as a man, and I saw neither meat nor drink wherewith to serve him; this was *one* marvel. *Another* marvel was, that this solemn lord had no servant but one, and him he sent out: I beheld, thinking what labour it may be that the servant should do; and then I understood that he should do the greatest labour, and the hardest travel; that is, he should be a gardner, delving and diking, and sweating, and turning the earth up and down, and seek the deepness, and water the plants in time: and in this he should continue his travel, and make sweatfloods to run, and noble plentuousness fruit to spring, which he should bring before the lord, and serve him therewith to his liking; and he should never turn again, till he had dight this meat all ready, as he knew that it liked to the lord: and then he should take this meat, with the drink, and bear it full worfully before the lord. And all this time the lord should sit right on the same place, abiding the servant whom he sent out. And yet I marvelled fro whence the servant came: for I saw in the lord, that he hath within himself endless life, and all manner of goodness, save the treasure that was in the earth: and that was grounded within the lord in marvellous deepness of endless love. But it was not all to his worship, till his servant hath thus nobly dight it, and brought it before him in himself present. And without the lord was right nought but wilderness. And I understood not all what this example meant; and therefore I marvelled from whence the servant came: in the servant is comprehended the Second Person of the Trinity; and in the servant is comprehended Adam; that is to say, all men. And therefore when I say the Son, it meaneth, the Godhead, which is even with the Father. And when I saw the servant, it meaneth Christs manhood, which is rightful Adam. By the nearhood of the servant, is understood the Son; and by the standing on the left side is understood Adam. The lord is God the Father: the servant is the Son, Jesu Christ: the Holy Ghost is the even love that is in them both. When Adam fell, Gods Son fell for the right oning which was made in heaven; Gods Son might not be separate from Adam, for by Adam I understand all man: Adam fell fro life to death into the slade of this wretched world; and after that into hell. Gods Son fell with Adam into the slade of the maidens womb; which was the fairest daughter of Adam; and that was for to excuse Adam from blame in heaven and in earth. And mightily he fetched him out of hell. By the wisdom and the goodness that was in the servant, is understood Gods Son; by the poor cloathing as a labourer standing near the left side, is understood the manhood of Adam, with all the mischief and feebleness that followeth: for in all this our good Lord shewed his own Son and Adam but one man. The vertue and the goodness that we have, is of Jesu Christ: the feebleness and blindness that we have, is of Adam; which *two* were shewed in the servant: and thus hath our good Lord Jesu taken upon him all our blame. And therefore our Father may nor will no more blame, assigne to us, than to his own dear worthy Son Jesu Christ. Thus was he the servant before his coming into the earth; standing ready before the Father in purpose, till what time he would send him to do the worshipful deed; by which mankind was brought again into heaven; that is to say, notwithstanding that he is God even with the Father, as anenst the Godhead: but in his fore-seeing purpose that he would be man, to save man in fulfilling of the will of his Father; so he stood before his Father as a servant, wilfully taking upon him all our charge. And then he start full readily at the Father's will; and anon he fell full low in the maidens womb, having no regard to himself, ne to his hard pains. The white kirtle is the flesh: the single-head is, that there was right nought between the God-head and the Man-hood: the straitness is poverty; the old is of Adams wearing; the defaulting is the sweat of Adams travel; the shortness sheweth the servant-labourer. And thus I saw the Son stand, saying in his meaning: '*Loe my dear Father, I stand before thee in Adams kirtle, all ready to start and to run; I would be in the earth to thy worship when it is thy will to send me, how long shall I desire it?*' Full truly wist the Son when it was the Fathers will; and how long he should desire; that is to say, as anenst the God-head, for he is the wisdom of the

Father. Wherefore this meaning was shewed in understanding of the manhood of Christ: for all mankind that shall be saved, by the sweet incarnation and passion of Christ, all is the manhood of Christ; for he is the head, and we be his members: to which members the day and the time is unknown, when every passing woe and sorrow shall have an end, and the everlasting joy and bliss shall be fulfilled. Which day and time for to see all the company of heaven longeth and desireth; and all that be under heaven, which shall come thither, their way is by longing and desiring. Which desiring and longing was shewed in the servant standing before the Lord; or else thus, in the Son standing before the Father in Adams kirtle: for the longing and desiring of all mankind that shall be safe appeared in Jesu; for Jesu is in all that may be safe, and all that be saved is in Jesu. And all of the charity of God, with obedience, meekness, and patience, and vertues that longeth to us. Also in this marvellous example, I have teaching within me, as it were the beginning of an A. B. C. whereby I may have some understanding of our Lords meaning: for the privities of the revelation be hid therein; notwithstanding that all the shewings be full of privities. The sitting of the Father betokeneth the God-head; that is to say, for shewing of rest and peace: for in the God-head may be no travel. And that he sheweth himself as lord, betokeneth to our manhood: the standing of the servant betokeneth travel:

and on the left side betokeneth, that he was not all worthy to stand even right before the lord. His starting was the God-head, and the running was the Man-head; for the God-head start fro the Father into the maidens womb, falling into the taking of our kind. And in this falling he took great sore: the sore that he took was our flesh, in which as soon as he took it, he had feeling of deadly pains. By that he stood dreadfull before the lord, and not even right, betokeneth that his cloathing was not honest to stand even right before the lord; nor that might not, nor should not be his office, whiles he was a labourer; nor also he might not sit with the lord in rest and peace, till he had won his peace rightfully with his hard travel. And by the left side that the Father left his own Son wilfully in the manhood, to suffer all mans pain without sparing of him. By that his kirtle was at the point to be ragged and rent; is understood the roddes and scourges, the thornes and the nails; the drawing and the dragging, his tender flesh renting, as I saw in some part, the tender flesh was rent from the head-pann, falling on pieces, unto the time the bleeding failed: and then it began to dry again, cleaving to the bone. And by the wallowing, and writhing, groaning, and mourning, is understood that he might never rise all mightily fro that time that he was fallen into the maidens womb, till his body was slain and dead, he yielding the soul into the Fathers hand, with all mankind for whom he was sent. And at this point he began first to shew his might; for then he went into hell. And when he was there, then he raised up the great root out of the deep deepness, which rightfully was knit to him in high heaven. The body lay in the grave till Easter morrow; and fro that time he lay never more, for there was rightfully ended the wallowing, and the writhing, the groaning, and the mourning. And our foul deadly flesh that Gods Son took upon him which was Adams old kirtle, strait, bare, and short, then by our Saviour was made fair, new, white, and bright, and of endless cleanness; wide, and side, fairer and richer than was the cloathing which I saw on the Father, for that cloathing was blew. And Christs cloathing is now of fair seemly medelour, which is so marvellous that I can it no descrie, for it is all of very worship. Now sitteth not the lord on earth in wilderness, but he sitteth on his rich and noble seat which he made in heaven most to his liking. Now standeth not the Son before the Father, as a servant before the lord, dreadfully cloathed in party naked: but he standeth before the Father even right richly cloathed, in blissful largeness; with a crown upon his head of precious richness: for it was shewed that we be his crown: which crown is the Fathers joy, the Sons worship, the Holy Ghosts liking; and endless marvellous bliss to all that be in heaven. Now standeth not the Son before the Father on the left side as a labourer; but he sitteth on the

Fathers right hand in endless rest and peace. But it is not meant that the Son sitteth on the right hand beside, as one man sitteth by another in this life: for there is no such sitting as to my sight in the Trinity; but he sitteth on his Fathers right hand; that is to say, right in the highest nobility of the Fathers joy. Now is the spouse Gods Son in peace with his loved wife: which is the fair maiden, of endless joy. Now sitteth the Son very God and very Man in his city in rest and in peace, which his Father hath dight to him of endless purpose: and the Father in the Son; and the Holy Ghost in the Father and in the Son.

The Fifty-second Chapter.

AND thus I saw that God enjoyeth that he is our father, and God enjoyeth that he is our mother: and God enjoyeth that he is our very spouse, and our soul his loved wife: And Christ enjoyeth that he is our brother: and Jesu enjoyeth that he is our Saviour. These be five high joyes, as I understand; in which he will that we enjoy, him praising, him thanking, him loving, him endlesly blessing, all that shall be saved, for the time of this life: we have in us a marvellous medelour both of weal and of woe: we have in us our Lord Jesu Christ up-risen; and we have in us the wretchedness and the mischief of Adams falling, dying. By Christ we be lastingly kept; and by his gracious touching we be raised into very trust of salvation. And by Adams falling, we be so briken in our feeling on diverse manners by sin and by sundry pains. In which we be made dark, and so blind, that unneths we can take any comfort. But in our meaning, we abide God, and faithfully trust to have mercy and grace. And this is his own working in us; and of his goodness openeth the eye of our understanding, by which we have sight, some time more, and sometime less, after that God giveth ability to take. And now we be raised into that one, and now we are suffered to fall into that other. And thus is that medle so marvellous in us, that unneths we know of our self, or of our even christen, in what way we stand for the marvellousness of this sundry feeling: but that each holy assent that we assent to God when we feel him, truly willing to be with him with all our heart, with all our soul, and with all our might. And then we hate and despise our evil stirring, and all that might be occasion of sin, ghostly and bodily. And yet nevertheless, when this sweetness is hid, we fall again into blindness, and so into woe and tribulation on diverse manners. But then is this our comfort, that we know in our faith that by the vertue of Christ which is our keeper, we assent never thereto. But we grudge there against, and endure in pain and in woe, praying into that time that he shewed him again to us. And thus we stand in this medelour all the dayes of our life: but he will we trust that he is lastingly with us; and that in *three* manners. He is with us in heaven very man, in his own person, us up-drawing: and that was shewed in the ghostly thirst. And he is with us in earth, us leading, and that was shewed in the *third;* where I saw God in a point. And he is with us in our soul, endlesly wonning, ruling, and guiding us: and that was shewed in the xvith. as I shall say. And thus in the servant was shewed the blindness and the mischief of Adams falling. And in the servant was shewed the wisdom and the goodness of Gods Son. And in the lord was shewed the rewth and the pity of Adams woe: and in the lord was shewed the high nobility and endless worship, that mankind is come to by the vertue of the passion and the death of his dear worthy Son. And therefore mightily he enjoyeth in his falling, for the high raising and fulhead of bliss that mankind is come to, over-passing that we should have had, if he had not fallen. And thus to see this over-passing nobility, was my understanding led into God, in the same time that I saw the servant fall. And thus we have matter of mourning; for our sin is cause of Christs pains: and we have lastingly matter of joy; for endless love made him to suffer. And therefore the creature that seeth and feeleth the working of love by grace, hateth nought but sin; for of all thing, as to my sight, love and hate be hardest and most unmeasurable contraries. And notwithstanding all this, I saw and understood this in our Lord's meaning, that we may not in this life keep us from sin; all holy in full cleanness, as we shall be in heaven. But we may well by grace keep us fro the sins which would lead us to endless pain, as Holy Church teacheth us, and eschew venial, reasonably up our might. And if we by our blindness, and our wretchedness any time fall, that we readily rise, knowing the sweet touching of grace; and wilfully amend us upon teaching of Holy Church after that the sin is grievous; and go forth with God in love: and neither on that one side fall over low, enclining to despair; ne on that other side be over richless, as we give no force: but meekly know our feebleness, witting that we may not stand the twinkling of an eye, but with keeping of grace; and reverently cleave to God, in him only trusting. For otherwise is the beholding of God, and otherwise is the beholding of man. For it longeth to man meekly to accuse himself; and it longeth to the proper goodness of our Lord God courteously to excuse man. And these be *two* parties that were shewed in the double chear, in which the Lord beheld the falling of his loved servant. *That one* was shewed outward, full meekly and mildly with great ruth and pity: and *that other* of inward endless love. And right thus will our good Lord that we accuse our self wilfully, and truly see and know his everlasting love that he hath to us, and his plentuous mercy. And thus graciously to see and know both together, is the meek accusing that our good Lord asketh of us: and himself worketh there it is; and this is the lower party of mans life. And it was shewed in the outward chear: in which shewing, I saw *two* parts. The *one* is the ruful falling of man: that *other* is the worshipful asseth that our Lord hath made for man. That other chear was shewed inward; and that was more highly and all one: for the life and the vertue that we have in the lower party is of the higher. And it cometh down to us of the kind love, of the self by grace. Between that one and that other is right naught; for it all is one love: which one blessed love hath now in us double working; for in the lower party be pains and passions, ruths and pities, mercies and forgiveness, and such other which be profitable. But in the higher party be none of these; but all one high love and marvellous joy: in which marvellous joy all pains be wholly destroyed. And in this not only our good Lord shewed our excusing; but also the worshipful nobility that he shall bring us to, turning all our blame into endless worship.

The Fifty-third Chapter.

AND thus I saw that he will that we know, that he taketh no harder the falling of any creature that shall be saved; then he took the falling of Adam, which we know was endlesly loved, and surely kept in the time of all his need; and now is blessedfully restored in high over-passing joyes. For our Lord God is so good, so gentle, and so courteous, that he may never assigne default final, in whom he shall be ever blessed and praised. And in this that I have now said, was my desire in party answered, and my great fear some deal eased by the lovely gracious shewing of our Lord God. In which shewing I saw and understood full surely, that in each soul that shall be safe, is a godly will that never assented to sin, ne never shall. Which will is so good that it may never will evil (finally): but evermore continually it willeth good, and worketh good in the sight of God. Wherefore our Lord will we know it in the faith and the belief: and namely and truly that we have all this blessed will whole and safe in our Lord Jesu Christ: for that each kind that heaven shall be fulfilled with, behooved needs of Gods rightfulness so to be knit and onid in him, that therein were kept a substance which might never, nor should be parted from him; and that through his own good will in his endless foresaid purpose. And notwithstanding this rightful knitting, and this endless oning, yet the redemption, and the again buying of mankind, is needful and speedful in every thing, as it is done for the same intent and the same end, that Holy Church in our faith us teacheth. For I saw that God began never to love mankind: for right, the same that mankind shall be in endless bliss (fulfilling the joy of God as anempts his works) right so the same mankind hath been in the foresight of God, known and loved fro without beginning in his rightful intent: and by the endless intent and assent, and the full accord of all the Trinity, the mid Person would be ground and head of this fair kind; out of whom we be all come, in whom we be all enclosed, into whom we shall all goe; in him finding our full heaven in everlasting joy, by the foreseeing purpose of all the blessed Trinity fro without beginning. For or that he made us he loved us; and when we were made, we loved him. And this is a love made of the kindly substancial goodness of the Holy Ghost; mightily in reason of the might of the Father, and wise, in mind of the wisdom of the Son. And thus is mans soul made of God; and in the same point knit to God. And thus I understood that mans soul is made of naught; that is to say, it is made, but of naught that is made; as thus: when God should make mans body, he took the slime of the earth, which is a matter medled and gathered of all bodily things; and thereof he made mans body. But to the making of mans soul, he would take right naught, but made it. And thus is the kind made rightfully oned to the Maker; which is substancial kind unmade, that is God. And therefore it is, that there may, ne shall be right naught between God and mans soul: and in this endless love mans soul is kept whole, as all the matter of the revelation meaneth and sheweth. In which endless love we be led and kept of God, and never shall be lost; for he will that we know that our soul is a life; which life of his goodness and his grace shall last in heaven without end, him loving, him thanking, him praising. And right the same that we should be without end, the same we were treasured in God, and hid, known, and loved fro without beginning. Wherefore he will we wit that the noblest thing that ever he made is mankind; and the fullest substance and the highest vertue is the blessed soul of Christ. And furthermore he will we wit, that this dear worthy soul was preciously knit to him in the making: which knot is so subtile and so mighty, that it is owned into God. In which oning it is made endlesly holy. Furthermore he will we wit that all the souls that shall be saved in heaven without end, be knit in this knot, and oned in this oning, and made holy in this holiness.

The Fifty-fourth Chapter.

AND for the great endless love that God hath to all mankind, he maketh no departing in love between the blessed soul of Christ, and the least soul that shall be saved: for it is full easie to believe and trust, that the dwelling of the blessed soul of Christ is full high in the glorious God-head. And truly as I understood in our Lords meaning; where the blessed soul of Christ is, there is the substance of all the souls that shall be saved by Christ, (in their exemplar and final cause.) Highly owe we to enjoy that God dwelleth in our soul; and more highly we owe to enjoy, that our soul dwelleth in God. Our soul is made to be Gods dwelling place; and the dwelling of our soul is God, which is unmade. A high understanding it is inwardly to see and to know that God which is our maker, dwelleth in our soul. And a higher understanding it is, and more inwardly, to see and to know our soul that is made dwelleth in God in substance: of which substance by God we be that we be. And I saw no difference between God and our substance, but as it were all God. And yet my understanding took, that our substance is in God; that is to say, that God is God, and our substance is a creature in God. For the almighty truth of the Trinity is our Father: for he made us, and keepeth us in him: and the deep wisdom of the Trinity is our mother, in whom we be closed: and the high goodness of the Trinity is our Lord, and in him we be closed, and he in us. We be closed in the Father, and we be closed in the Son, and we be closed in the Holy Ghost. And the Father is beclosed in us; the Son is beclosed in us; and the Holy Ghost is beclosed in us: all might, all wisdom, and all goodness, one God, one Lord. And our faith is a vertue that cometh of our kind substance into our sensual soul by the Holy Ghost. In which vertue all our vertues come into us; for without that, no man may receive vertues; for it is naught else but a right understanding, with true beleif, and sure trust of our being that we be in God, and he in us, which we see not. And this vertue with all others that God hath ordained to us coming therein, worketh in us great things; for Christ mercifully is working in us; and we graciously according to him through the gift and the vertue of the Holy Ghost. This working maketh that we be Christs children, and christen in lyving.

The Fifty-fifth Chapter.

And thus Christ is our way, us surely leading in his laws. And Christ in his body mightily beareth us up into heaven. For I saw that Christ, us all having in him that shall be saved by him, worshipfully presenteth his Father in heaven with us; which present full thankfully his Father receiveth, and courteously giveth it unto his Son Jesu Christ. Which gift and working is joy to the Father, and bliss to the Son, and liking to the Holy Ghost. And of all thing that to us longeth, it is most liking to our Lord that we enjoy in this joy, which is in the blessed Trinity of our salvation. And this was seen in the *ninth* shewing, where it speaketh more of this matter. And notwithstanding all our feeling, woe or weal, God will we understand and believe, that we be more verily in heaven, than in earth. Our faith cometh of the kind love of our soul, and of the clear light of our reason, and of the stedfast mind which we have of God in our first making. And what time our soul is inspired in our body, in which we be made sensual, assoon mercy and grace begin to work; having of us cure and keeping with pity and love. In which working the Holy Ghost formeth in our faith hope, that we shall come again up above to our substance into the vertue of Christ, encreased and fulfilled through the Holy Ghost. Thus I understood that the sensuality is grounded in kind, in mercy and in grace: which ground ableth us to receive gifts that lead us to endless life; for I saw full surely that our substance is in God. And also I saw that in our sensuality God is; for in the same point that our soul is made sensual, in the same point is the city of God ordained to him from without beginning. In which city he cometh, and never shall remove it; for God is never out of the soul, in which he shall dwell blessedly without end. And this was said in the xvith. shewing, where it saith, "The place that Jesu taketh in our soul, he shall never remove it." And all the gifts that God may give to the creature, he hath given to his Son Jesu for us. Which gifts he wonning in us hath beclosed in him, into the time that we be waxen and grown, our soul with our body, and our body with our soul; either of them take help of other till we be brought up into stature, as kind worketh. And then in the ground of kind, with working of mercy, the Holy Ghost graciously enspireth into us gifts leading to endless life. And thus was my understanding led of God to see in him, and to wit, to understand and to know, that our soul is a made Trinity, like to the unmade blessed Trinity, known and loved from without beginning; and in the making oned to the Maker, as it is before said. This sight was full sweet and marvellous to behold, peaceable and restful, sure and delectable. And for the worshipful oning that was thus made of God, between the soul and the body, it behooved needs to be, that mankind should be restored fro double death: which restoring might never be into the time that the second Person in the Trinity had taken the lower party of mankind; to whom that highest was oned in the first making. And these two parties were in Christ, the higher and the lower, which is but one soul: the higher party was ever in peace with God in full joy and bliss: the lower party, which is sensuality, suffered for the salvation of mankind. And these two parties were seen and felt in the viiith. shewing; in which my body was fulfilled of feeling, and mind of Christs passion, and his dying. And furthermore, with this was a subtile feeling and a privy inward sight of the high parts. And that was shewed in the same time, where I might not for the mean profer look up into heaven: and that was for that each mighty beholding of the inward life: which inward life is that high substance that precious soul which is endless enjoying in the God-head.

The Fifty-sixth Chapter.

AND thus I saw full surely that it is ready to us, and more easie, to come to the knowing of God, than to know our own soul. For our soul is so deep grounded in God, and so endlesly treasured, that we may not come to the knowing thereof, till we have first knowing of God; which is the Maker to whom it is oned. But notwithstanding, I saw that we have kindly of fulhead to desire wisely and truly to know our own soul, whereby we be learned to seek it there it is, and that is into God. And thus by the gracious leading of the Holy Ghost we shall know him both in one. Whether we be stirred to know God or our soul, it is both good and true. God is more nearer to us than our own soul; for he is ground in whom our soul standeth, and he is mean that keepeth the substance and the sensuality together, so that it shall never depart: for our soul sitteth in God in very rest, and our soul standeth in God in sure strength: and our soul is kindly rooted in God in endless love. And therefore if we will have knowing of our soul, and commoning, and daliance therewith, it behooveth to seek into our Lord God, in whom it is inclosed. And of this enclosing, I saw and understood more in the xvith shewing, as I shall say. And as aneinst our substance it may rightly be called our soul: and aneinst our sensuality it may rightly be called our soul; and that is by the oning that it hath in God. That worshipful city that our Lord Jesu sitteth in it is our sensuality in which he is enclosed. And our kindly substance is beclosed in Jesu, with the blessed soul of Christ sitting in rest in the God-head. And I saw full surely that it behooveth needs to be, that we should be in longing, and in penance, into the time that we be led so deep into God; that we verily and truly know our own soul. And surely I saw, that into this high deepness our good Lord himself leadeth us in the same love that he made us, and in the same love he bought us by mercy and grace, through vertue of his blessed passion; and notwithstanding all this, we may never come to the full knowing of God, till we know first clearly our own soul; for into the time that it is in the full mights, we may not be all holy; and that is, that our sensuality by the vertue of Christs passion, be brought up into the substance, with all the profits of our tribulation that our Lord shall make us to get by mercy and grace. I had in party touching, and it is grounded in kind; that is to say, our reason is grounded in God, which is substancially kindness. Of this substancial kindness, mercy and grace springeth, and spreadeth into us, working all things in fulfilling of our joy. These be our grounds in which we have our being, our encrease, and our fulfilling; for in kind, we have our life and our being; and in mercy and grace, we have our encrease and our fulfilling. It be *three* properties in one goodness: and where that one worketh all worken in the thing that belongen to us. God will we understand, desiring with all our heart, and with all our strength, to have knowing of them ever more and more, into the time that we be fulfilled. For fully to know them, and clearly to see them is not else but endless joy and bliss that we shall have in heaven, which God will we begin here in knowing of his love; for only by our reason we may not profit: but if we have evenly therewith mind and love: ne only in our kindly ground that we have in God, we may not be saved, but if we have, coming of the same ground, mercy and grace. For of these three workings, altogether we receive all our goods; of which, the first be goods of kind. For in our first making, God gave us as much good, and as great good, as we might receive only in our spirit: but his fore-seeing purpose in his endless wisdom, would that we were double.

The Fifty-seventh Chapter.

AND against our substance, he made us so noble, and so rich, that evermore we work his will and his worship; there I say, we, it meaneth man that shall be saved. For truly I saw that we be that he loveth, and do that him liketh, lastingly without any stinting. And of this, great riches; and of this, high noble vertues by measure come to our soul, what time that it is knit to our body: in which knitting we be made sensual. And thus in our substance we be full, and in our sensuality we fail; which failing God will restore and fulfill by working of mercy and grace, plenteously flowing into us of his own kind goodness. And thus this kind goodness maketh that mercy and grace worketh in us. And the kind goodness that we have of him, ableth us to receive the working of mercy and grace. I saw that our kind is in God whole; in which he maketh diversities flowing out of him to work his will; whose kind keepeth, and mercy and grace restoreth and fulfilleth. And of these none shall be perished; for our kind which is the higher party, is knit to God in the making, and God is knit to our kind, which is the lower party in our flesh taking. And thus in Christ our two kinds be oned: for the Trinity is comprehended in Christ, in whom our higher party is grounded and rooted; and our lower party the second Person hath taken, which kind first to him was a dight. For I saw full truly, that all the works that God hath done, or ever shall, were full known to him, and before seen fro without beginning. And for love he made mankind; and for the same love himself would become man. The next good that we receive is our faith, in which our profiting beginneth; and it becometh of the high riches of our kind substance into our sensual soul; and it is grounded in us, and we in that, through the kind goodness of God, by the working of mercy and grace. And thereof come all our goods, by which we be led and saved; for the commandments of God come therein: in which we owe to have *two* manner of understanding: *that one* is, that we owe to understand and know which be his bidings, to love them, and to keep them. *That other* is, that we owe to know his forbiddings, to hate them, and to refuse them: for in these two is all our working comprehended. Also in our faith come the seven sacraments, each following other in order as God hath ordained them to us, and all manner vertues; for the same vertues that we have received of our substance given to us in kind of the goodness of God, the same vertues by the working of mercy be given to us in grace through the Holy Ghost renewed: which vertues and gifts are treasured to us in Jesu Christ; for in that same time that God knit him to our body in the maidens womb, he took our sensual soul. In which taking he, us all having beclosed in him, he oned it to our substance. In which oning he was perfect man; for Christ having knit in him all man that shall be saved, is perfect man. Thus our Lady is our mother, in whom we be all beclosed, and of her born in Christ; for she that is mother of our Saviour, is mother of all that be saved in our Saviour. And our Saviour is our very mother, in whom we be endlesly born, and never shall come out of him. Plentuously, fully, and sweetly was this shewed: and it is spoken of in the *first*, where it is said, "We be all in him beclosed, and he is beclosed in us." And that is spoken of in the xvith. shewing, where he saith, "*He sitteth in our soul;*" for it is his liking to reign in our understanding blessedfully, and sitteth in our soul restfully: and to dwell in our soul endlesly, us all working into him. In which working he will we be his helpers, giving to him all our intent, learning his laws, keeping his lore, desiring that all bedone that he doth, truly trusting in him; for verily I saw that all our substance is in God.

The Fifty-eighth Chapter.

God the blessedful Trinity which is everlasting being, right as he is endless from without beginning; right so it was in his purpose endless to make mankind. Which fair kind was first dight to his own Son the Second Person; and when he would by full accord of all the Trinity, he made us all at ones. And in our making he knit us, and oned us to himself: by which oning, we be kept as clean, and as noble as we were made; by the vertue of that each precious oning, we love our Maker, and like him, praise him, and thank him, and endlesly enjoy in him. And this is the working which is wrought continually in each soul that shall be saved: which is the godly will before said. And thus in our making God Almighty is our kindly Father. And God all wisdom is our kindly mother, with the love and the goodness of the Holy Ghost, which is all one God, one Lord. And in the knitting, and in the oning he is our very true spouse, and we his loved wife, and his fair maiden; with which wife he was never displeased, for he saith, '*I love thee, and thou lovest me, and our love shall never part in two.*' I beheld the working of all the blessed Trinity. In which beholding, I saw and understood these *three* properties; the property of the father-head, and the property of the mother-head, and the property of the lordship in one God. In our Father Almighty we have our keeping, and our bliss. And aneynst our kindly substance, which is to us by our making fro without beginning. And in the Second Person, in wit and wisdom we have our keeping: and aneynst our sensuality, our restoring, and our saving;

for he is our Mother, Brother, and Saviour. And in our good Lord the Holy Ghost we have our rewarding, and our yielding for our living and our travel, and endlesly over-passing all that we desire in his marvellous courtesie of his high plentuous grace; for all our life is in *three:* in the *first* our being: and in the *second*, we have our encreasing: and in the *third*, we have our fulfilling. The *first* is kind; the *second* is mercy; the *third* is grace. For the *first*, I saw and understood, that the high might of the Trinity is our Father, and the deep wisdom of the Trinity is our Mother, and the great love of the Trinity is our Lord. And all these have we in kind, and in our substantial making. And furthermore, I saw that the Second Person which is our Mother substancially, the same deer worthy person is now become our mother sensual; for we be double of Gods making; that is to say, substancial and sensual. Our substance is the higher party which we have in our Father God Almighty: and the Second Person of the Trinity is our Mother in kind, in our substancial making, in whom we be grounded and rooted: and he is our Mother of mercy, in our sensuality taking. And thus our Mother is to us diverse manner working, in whom our parts be kept undeparted: for in our Mother Christ we profit and encrease; and in mercy he reformeth us and restoreth. And by the vertue of his passion, his death, and his uprising oned us to our substance. This worketh our Mother in mercy to all his beloved children, which be to him buxom and obedient: and grace worketh with mercy, and namely in *two* properties, as it was shewed. Which working longeth to the Third Person the Holy Ghost; he worketh rewarding and giving. Rewarding is a gift of trust that the Lord doth to them that hath traveled. And giving is a courteous working which he doth freely of grace, fulfilling and over-passing all that is deserved of creatures. Thus in our Father God Almighty we have our being. And in our Mother of mercy Jesu Christ, we have our reforming, and our restoring, in whom our parts be oned, and all made perfect man: and by yielding and giving in grace of the Holy Ghost we be fulfilled, and our substance is in our Father, God Almighty: and our substance is in our Mother God all wisdom: and our substance is in our Lord God the Holy Ghost, all goodness; for our substance is whole in each person of the Trinity, which is one God. And our sensuality is only in the Second Person, Christ Jesu, in whom is the Father and the Holy Ghost. And in him, and by him, we be mightily taken out of hell, and out of the wretchedness in earth; and worshipfully brought up into heaven, and blessedfully oned to our substance; encreased in riches and nobly, by all the vertue of Christ, and by the grace and working of the Holy Ghost.

The Fifty-ninth Chapter.

AND all this bliss we have by mercy and grace: which manner bliss we might never have had and known; but if that property and goodness which is in God had been contraried, whereby we have this bliss: for wickedness hath been suffered to rise contrary to that goodness; and the goodness of mercy and grace contraried against that wickedness; and turned all to goodness and worship to all that shall be saved: for it is that property in God which doth good against evil. Thus Jesu Christ that doth good against evil is our very Mother. We have our being of him, where the ground of Mother-head beginneth, with all the sweet keeping of love that endlesly followeth. As verily as God is our Father; as verily is God our Mother; and that shewed he in all; and namely, in these sweet words there he saith, '*I it am;*' that is to say, '*I it am, the might and the goodness of the Father-head: I it am, the wisdom and the kindness of the Mother-head: I it am, the light and the grace, that is all blessed love: I it am, the Trinity: I it am, the Unity: I it am, the high sovereign goodness of all manner thing: I it am, that maketh thee to long: I it am, the endless fulfilling of all true desires.*' For there the soul is highest, noblest, and worshipfullest, yet it is lowest, meekest, and mildest. And of this substancioal ground we have all our vertues in our sensuality by gift of kind, and by helping, and speeding of mercy and grace; without which we may not profit. Our high Father Almighty God, which is being, he knoweth us, and loved us fro before any time. Of which knowing in his full marvellous deep charity, by the fore-seeing endless counsel of all the blessed Trinity; he would that the Second Person should become our Mother, our Brother, and our Saviour. Whereof it followeth, that as verily as God is our Father, verily God is our Mother. Our Father willeth, our Mother worketh. Our good Lord the Holy Ghost confirmeth; and therefore it longeth to us to love our God in whom we have our being, him reverently thanking and praising of our making, mightily praying to our Mother of mercy and pity, and to our Lord the Holy Ghost, of help and grace: for in these three is all our life, kind, mercy, and grace: whereof we have mild-head, patience and pity, and hating of sin and wickedness, for it longeth properly to vertues to hate sin and wickedness. And thus is Jesu our very Mother in kind of our first making: and he is our very first Mother in grace by taking of our kind made; all the fair working, and all the sweet kindly offices of dear worthy Mother-head is impropred to the Second Person: for in him we have this goodly will whole and safe without end, both in kind and in grace, of his own proper goodness. I understood *three* manner of beholdings of Mother-head in God. The *first* is, ground of our kind making. The *second* is, taking of our kind, and there beginneth the Mother-head of grace. The *third* is, Mother-head in working: and therein is a forth-speeding by the same grace; of length, and bredth, of height and of deepness without end, and all is one love.

The Sixtieth Chapter.

BUT now me behooveth to see a little more of this forth-spreading, as I understood in the meaning of our Lord; how that we be brought again by the Mother-head of mercy and grace into our kindly steed, where that we were in made by the Mother-head of kind love; which kind love never leaveth us. Our kind Mother, our gracious Mother; for he would all whole become our Mother in all thing; he took the ground of his work full low, and full mildly in the maidens womb. And that shewed he in the first, where he brought the meek maiden before the eye of my understanding, in the simple stature as she was when he conceived; that is to say, our high God the severeign wisdom of all. In this low place he arraid him, and dight him all ready in our poor flesh, himself to do the service and the office of Mother-hood in all thing. The Mothers service is nearest, readiest and surest. Nearest, for it is most of kind; readiest, for it is most of love; and sikerest, for it is most of truth. This office, ne might, nor could never none done to the full, but he alone. We wit that all our mothers bear us to pain and to dying. What is that but our very Mother Jesu? He alone beareth us to joy, and to endless living, blessed mote he be. Thus he sustained us within him, in love and travel, into the full time that he would suffer the sharpest thornes, and grievous pains that ever were, or ever shall be, and died at the last. And when he had done, and so borne us to bliss, yet might not all this make asseeth to his marvellous love. And that he shewed in these high over-passing words of love; '*If I might suffer more I would suffer more.*' He might no more die, but he would not stint working. Wherefore him behooveth to find us, for the dear worthy love of mother-hood hath made him debtor to us. The mother may give her child to suck her milk; but our precious Mother Jesu he may feed us with himself, and doth full courteously, and full tenderly with the blessed sacrament; that is precious food of very life, and with all the sweet sacraments he sustaineth us full mercifully, and graciously. And so meant he in these blessed words, where he said, '*I it am that Holy Church preacheth thee, and teacheth thee;*' that is to say, all the health and the life of the sacraments; all the vertue and the grace of my word; all the goodness that is ordained in Holy Church to thee; '*I it am.*' The mother may lay her child tenderly to her breast; but our tender Mother Jesu he may homely lead us into his blessed breast by his sweet open side, and shew us there in party of the Godhead, and the joyes of heaven, with ghostly sureness of endless bliss. And that shewed he in the ixth. Revelation, giving the same understanding in this sweet word, where he saith, '*Loe how I love thee;*' behold into his blessed side enjoying. This fair lovely word, Mother, it is so sweet and so kind in it self, that it may not verily be said of none, ne to none but of him, and to him, that is very Mother of life and of all. To the property of Mother-head longeth kind love, wisdom, and knowing; and it is God: for though it be so, that our bodily forth-bringing be but little, low, and simple, in regard of our ghostly forth-bringing, yet it is he that doth it in the creatures, by whom that it is done. The kind loving mother that wotteth, and knoweth the need of her child, she keepeth it full tenderly, as the kind and condition of mother-head will; and ever as it waxeth in age and in stature, she changeth the works, but not her love: and when it is waxed of more age, she suffereth that it be chastised; in breaking down of vices, to make the child receive vertues and grace. This working with all that be fair and good, our Lord doth it in him by whom it is done. Thus he is our Mother in kind by the working of grace in the lower party, for love of the higher. And he will that we know it; for he will have all our love fastned to him. And in this I saw that all debt that we owe by Gods bidding to Father-head and Mother-head, is fulfilled in true loving of God: which blessed love Christ worketh in us. And this was shewed in all; and namely, in the high plentuous words, where he saith; '*I it am that thou lovest.*'

The Sixty-first Chapter.

And in our ghostly forth-bringing he useth more tenderness in keeping, without any comparison; by as much as our soul is of more price in his sight: he kindleth our understanding; he prepareth our wayes; he easeth our conscience; he comforteth our soul; he lighteth our heart, and giveth us in party knowing, and loving in his blessedful God-head, with gracious mind in his sweet Man-hood, and his blessed passion; with courteous marvelling in his high over-passing goodness; and maketh us to love all that he loveth for his love, and to be well apaid with him, and with all his works. And when we fall hastily, he raiseth us by his lovely beclipping, and his gracious touching. And when we be strengthened by his sweet working, then we wilfully choose him by his grace, to be his servants, and his lovers, lastingly without end. And yet after this he suffereth some of us to fall more hard, and more grievous than ever we did before, as us thinketh. And then wene we that we be not all wise, that all were naught that we have begun, but it is not so: for it needeth us to fall, and it needeth us to see it; for if we fell not, we should not know how feeble, and how wretched we be of our self, nor also we should not so fulsomely know the marvellous love of our Maker; for we shall verily see in heaven without end, that we have grievously sinned in this life. And notwithstanding this, we shall verily see that we were never hurt in his (eternal) love, nor we were never the less of price in his sight. And by the assey of this falling, we shall have an high and a marvellous knowing of love in God without end: for hard and marvellous is that love which may not, nor will not be broken for trespass. And this was one understanding of profit. Another is the lowness and meekness that we shall get by the sight of our falling; for thereby we shall highly be raised in heaven: to which rising we might never have come without that meekness. And therefore it needed us to see it; and if we see it not, though we feel it, it should not profit us. And commonly first we fall, and sithen we see it, and both is of the mercy of God. The mother may suffer the child to fall some time, and be diseased in diverse manners for the own profit; but she may never suffer that any manner of peril come to her child, for love.

And though our earthly mother may suffer her child to perish, our heavenly Mother Jesu may never suffer us that be his children to perish; for he is all mighty, all wisdom, and all love: and so is none but he, blessed mote he be. But ofttimes when our falling and our wretchedness is shewed us, we be sore adread, and so greatly ashamed of our self, that unneths we wit where that we may hold us. But then will not our courteous Mother that we flee away: for him were nothing lother. But he will then that we use the condition of a child: for when it is diseased and afraid, it runneth hastily to the mother; and if it may do no more, it crieth on the mother for help, with all the might; so will he that we done as the meek child, saying thus: 'My kind Mother, my gracious Mother, my dear worthy Mother, have mercy upon me; I have made myself foul, and unlike to thee, and I may not, nor can amend it, but with thine help and grace.' And if we feel us not than eased assoon, be we sure that he useth the condition of a wise mother: for if he see that it be for profit to us to mourn and to weep, he suffereth with ruth and pity into the best time for love. And he will then that we use the property of a child, that evermore kindly trusteth to the love of the mother, in weal and in woe. And he will that we take us mightily to the faith of Holy Church, and find there our dear worthy Mother in solace and true understanding, with all the blessed common: for one singular person may oftentimes be broken, as it seemeth to the self, but the whole body of Holy Church was never broken, ne never shall be without end. And therefore a sure thing it is, a good and a gracious, to will meekly, and mightily be fastened and oned to our Mother Holy Church, that is Christ Jesu. For the flood of mercy; that is his dear worthy blood and precious water is plentuous to make us fair and clean. The blessed wounds of our Saviour be open and enjoy to heal us. The sweet gracious hands of our Mother be ready and diligent about us; for he in all this working useth the very office of a kind nurse that hath naught else to done, but to entend to the salvation of her child. It is his office to save us; it is his worship to do it; and it is his will we know it: for he will we love him sweetly, and trust in him meekly and mightily. And this shewed he in these gracious words, '*I keep thee full surely.*'

The Sixty-second Chapter.

For in that time he shewed our frailty and our fallings, our breakings and our naughtings, our despites and our chargings, and all our woe, as far forth as me thought that it might fall in this life. And therewith he shewed his blessed might, his blessed wisdom, his blessed love, that he keepeth us in this time as tenderly, and as sweetly to his worship, and as surely to our salvation, as he doth when we be in most solace and comfort. And thereto raiseth us ghostly and highly in heaven, and turneth all to his worship, and to our joy without end. For his precious love he suffereth us never to loose time, (since all things turn to our greater good.) And all this is of the kind goodness of God by the working of grace. God is kind in his being; that is to say, that goodness that is kind, it is God; he is the ground, he is the substance, he is the same thing that is kindness: and he is very Father and very Mother of kinds: and all kinds that he hath made to flow out of him to work his will, it should be restored and brought again into him by salvation of man, through the working of grace. For of all kinds that he hath set in divers creatures by party, in man is all the whole in ful head; and in vertue, in fairhead, and in good-head, in rialty and in noblety, in all manner of solemnity of preciousness and worship. Here may we see that we be all bound to God for kind, and we be bound to God for grace. Here may we see that us needeth not greatly to seek far out to know sundry kinds, but to Holy Church into our Mothers breast; that is to say, into our own soul, where our Lord dwelleth: and there should we find all now, in faith and in understanding; and after verily in himself clearly in bliss. But no man, ne woman take this singularity to himself; for it is not so, it is general: for it is our precious Mother Christ, and to him was this fair kind dight, for the worship and the nobly of mans making, and for the joy and the bliss of mans salvation, right as he saw, wist and knew from without beginning.

The Sixty-third Chapter.

HERE may we see that we have verily of kind to hate sin. And we have verily of grace to hate sin, for kind is all good and fair in itself: and grace was sent out to save kind, and keep kind, and destroy sin, and bring again fair kind into the blessed point fro thence it came; that is, God, with more nobleness and worship by the vertuous working of grace; for it shall be seen before God, of all his holy in joy without end, that kind hath been assaid in the fire of tribulation, and therein found no lack, nor no default. Thus is kind and grace of one accord; for grace is God, as unmade kind is God: he is two in manner working, and one in love. And neither of them worketh without other, ne none be departed. And when we by the mercy of God, and with his help accord us to kind and to grace, we shall see verily that sin is worse, viler and painfuller than hell, without any likeness: for it is contrarious to our fair kind; for as verily as sin is unclean, as truly sin is unkind. And this is an horrible thing to see, to the loving soul that would be all fair and shining in the sight of God, as kind and grace teacheth. But be we not adread of this, but in as much as dread may speed; but meekly make we our moan to our dear worthy Mother, and he shall all besprinckle us in his precious blood, and make our soul full soft, and full mild, and heal us full fair by process of time, right as it is most worship to him, and joy to us without end. And of this sweet fair working he shall never cease nor stint, till all his dear worthy children be brought forth and born. And that shewed he where he gave the understanding of the ghostly thirst; that is, the love-longing that shall last till doomes-day. Thus in our very Mother Jesu our life is grounded in the fore-seeing wisdom of himself fro without beginning, with the high might of the Father, and the sovereign goodness of the Holy Ghost. And in the taking of our kind he quicked us; and in his blessed dying upon the cross he bare us to endless life. And fro that time, and now and ever shall into doomes-day, he feedeth us and fordreth us, right as the high sovereign kindness of Mother-head will, and as the kindly need of child-head asketh. Fair and sweet is our heavenly Mother Jesu in the sight of our soul; precious and lovely be the gracious children in the sight of our heavenly Mother: with mildness and meekness, and all that fair vertues that long to children in kind; for kindly the child dispaireth not of the mothers love; kindly the child presumeth not of it self; kindly the child loveth the mother, and each one of them other. These be as fair vertues with all other that be like, wherewith our heavenly Mother is served and pleased. And I understood none higher stature in this life than child-hood in feebleness, and failing of might and of wit, into the time our gracious Mother hath brought us up into that our Fathers bliss. And there shall it verily be made known to us, his meaning in the sweet words, where he saith, '*All shall be well, and thou shalt see it thy self that all manner of thing shall be well.*'

The Fifteenth Revelation.

The Sixty-fourth Chapter.

AND then shall the bliss of our Mother-head in Christ be new to begin in the joyes of our Father God: which new beginning shall last without end. Now beginning thus, I understood, that all his blessed children which be come out of him by kind, should be brought into him again by grace. Afore this time I had great longing and desire of Gods gift to be delivered of this world, and of this life; for oft-times I beheld the woe that is here, and the weal and the blessed being that is there. And if there had no pain been in this life, but the absence of our Lord, methought sometime that it was more than I might bear. And this made me to mourn and busily to long. And also of my own wretchedness, slouth and weariness that me liked, not to live and to travel as me fell to do. And to all this our courteous Lord answered for comfort and patience, and said these words: '*Suddenly thou shalt be taken from all thy pain, from all thy sickness, from all thy disease, and from all thy woe. And thou shalt come up above, and thou shalt have me to thy meed, and thou shalt be fulfilled of joy and bliss; and thou shalt never more have no manner of pain, no manner of sickness, no manner misliking, no wanting of will, but ever joy and bliss without end. What should it then grieve thee to suffer a while, sithen it is my will and my worship?*' And in this word *(suddenly thou shalt be taken)* I saw that God rewarded man of the patience that he hath in abiding of Gods will, and of his time. And that man lengeth his patience over the time of his living; for unknowing the time of his passing. This is a great profit; for if a man knew his time, he should not have patience over that time. And also God will that while the soul is in the body, it seem to it self that it is ever at the point to be taken (out thereof,) for all this life and this longing that we have here is but a point. And when we be taken suddenly out of pain into bliss, then pain shall be nought. And in this time I saw a body lying on the earth: which body shewed heavy and fearful, and without shape and form, as it were a swilge stinking myre. And suddenly out of this body sprung a full fair creature, a little child full shapen and formed, swift and lively, and whiter than the lilly, which sharply glided up into heaven. The swilge of the body betokeneth great wretchedness of our deadly flesh: and the littleness of the child betokeneth the cleanness and the pureness of our soul. And I thought with this body bliveth no fairness of this child, ne of this child dwelleth no foulness of this body. It is full bliss-ful (for) man to be taken from pain, more than pain to be taken from man; for if pain be taken from us, it may come again. Therefore this is a sovereign comfort, and a bless-ful beholding in a longing soul, that we shall be taken from pain; for in this behest I saw a merciful compassion that our Lord hath in us for our woe, and a courteous behighting of clear deliverance: for he will that we be comforted in the over-passing joy. And that he shewed in these words; '*And thou shalt come up above; and thou shalt have me to thy meed, and thou shalt be fulfilled of joy and bliss.*' It is Gods will that we set the point of our thought in this blissful beholding as oft-time as we may, and as long time keep us therein with his grace; for this is a blissful contemplation to the soul that is led of God, and full much to his worship for the time that it lasteth. And when we fall again to our self by heaviness and ghostly blindness, and feeling of pains ghostly and bodily by our fragility: it is Gods will that we know, that he hath not forget us. And so meaneth he in these words, and saith for comfort; '*And thou shalt never more have pain in no manner; nor no manner of sickness, no manner of mis-liking, no want of will, but ever joy and bliss without end: what should it then agrieved thee to suffer a while, sithen it is my will and my worship?*' It is Gods will that we take his behests and his comfortings as largely and as mightily as we may take them. And also he will that we take our abidings and our diseases as lightly as we may take them, and set them at naught: for the lightlier that we take them, and the less price that we set at them for love, less pain shall we have in the feeling of them, and the more thank and meed shall we have for them.

The Sixty-fifth Chapter.

AND thus I understood that what man or woman wilfully choseth God in this life for love, he may be sure that he is loved without end, with endless love that worketh in him that grace; for he will we keep this trustily, that we be as sicker in hope of the bliss of heaven whiles we are here, as we shall be in surety when we are there. And ever the more liking and joy that we take in this sickerness, with reverence and meekness, the better liketh him.

For as it was shewed, this reverence that I mean, is a holy, courteous dread of our Lord, to which meekness is knit; and that is, that a creature see the Lord marvellous great, and her self marvellous litle: for these vertues are had endlesly to the loved of God. And it may now be seen and felt in measure by the gracious presence of our Lord, when it is: which presence in all thing is most desired; for it worketh that marvellous sickerness in true faith, and siker hope by greatness of charity in dread that is sweet and delectable. It is Gods will that I see my self as much bound to him in love, as if he had done for me all that he hath done. And thus should every soul think in regard of his love; that is to say, the charity of God maketh in us such a unity, that when it is truly seen no man can part them self from other. And thus ought each soul to think that God hath done for him all that he hath done. And this sheweth he to make us to love him, and liken him, and nothing dread but him; for it is his will we know that all the might of our enemies is locked in our friends hands. And therefore the soul that knoweth this sickerly, he shall not dread but him that she loveth. All other dreads she set them among passions, and bodily sickness, and imaginations. And therefore though we been in so much pain, woe and disease that us thinketh, we can think right naught but that we are in, or that we feel; assoon as we may we pass it lightly over, and set we it at naught. And why? for

God will be known; for if we know him, and love him, and reverently dread him, we shall have patience, and be in great rest. And it should been great liking to us all that he doth. And this shewed our Lord in these words: '*What should it then agrieve thee to suffer a while, seeing it is my will and my worship?*' Now have I told you of xv. Shewings, as God witsafe to minister them to my mind, renewed by lightnings and touchings, I hope, of the same Spirit that sheweth them all. Of which xv. shewings the *first* began early in the morning, about the hour of four; and it lasted shewing by process full fair and soberly, each following other till it was noon of the day, or past.

The Sixteenth Revelation.

The Sixty-sixth Chapter.

AND after this the good Lord shewed the xvith. Revelation on the night following, as I shall say after. Which xvith. was conclusion and confirmation to all the xv. But first me behooveth to tell you as anenst my feebleness, wretchedness and blindness. I have said at the beginning where it saith (*And in this suddenly all my pain was taken from me.*) Of which pain I had no grief, ne no disease, as long as the xv. Shewings lasted in shewing. And at the end all was close, and I saw no more; and soon I felt that I should live longer. And anon my sickness came again; first in my head with a sound and a noise: and suddenly all my body was fulfilled with sickness, like as it was before. And I was as barren and as dry as I had never had comfort but litle, and as a wretch mourned heavily for feeling of my bodily pains, and for faulting of comfort ghostly and bodily. Then came a religious person unto me and asked me how I fared; and I said, 'I had raved to day,' and he laught lowd and inwardly. And I said, 'The cross that stood before my face, methought it bled fast.' And with this word the person that I spake to waxed all sad and marvelled. And anon I was sore ashamed, and astonished for my retchlesness. And I thought this man taketh sadly the least word that I may say, that saw no more thereof. And when I saw that he took it so sadly, and with so great reverence, I waxed full greatly ashamed, and would have been shriven, but I could tell it to no Priest; for I thought, 'How should a Priest believe me, when I by saying I raved, I shewed myself not to believe our Lord God.' Notwithstanding, I believed him truly for the time that I saw him. And so was then my will and my meaning ever for to doe without end; but as a fool I let it pass out of my mind. Ah, Loe how wretched I was; this was a great sin and a great unkindness, that I for folly of feeling of a litle bodily pain, so unwisely left for the time the comfort of all this blessed shewing of our Lord God. Here may you see what I am of myself. But herein would our courteous Lord not leave me. And I lay still till night trusting in his mercy; and then I began to sleep.

The Sixty-seventh Chapter.

AND in my sleep at the beginning, methought the fiend set him in my throat, putting forth a visage full near my face, like a young man: and it was long and wonder lean, I saw never none such. The colour was red like the tile stone when it is new brent, with black spots therein, like frackles, fouler than the tile-stone; his hair was red, as rust not scoured; afore with side locks hanging down in flakes; he grinned upon me with a shrowd look, and shewed me white teeth: and so my kill me thought it the more ugly; body, ne hands had he none, shapely; but with his paws he held me in the throat, and would have stopped my breath, and kild me, but he might not. This ugly shewing was made sleeping, and so was none other. And in all this time I trusted to be saved and kept by the mercy of God. And our courteous Lord gave me grace to wake, and unnethes had any life. The persons that were with me beheld me, and wet my temples, and my heart began to comfort. And anon a little smoke came in at the door, with a great heat, and a foul stinch; and then I said, 'Benedicite dominus, Is it all on fire that is here?' And I went it had been a bodily fire, that should burn us all to death? I asked them that were with me, if they felt any stench, they said nay, they felt none; I said, 'Blessed be God,' for then wist I well it was the fiend that was come only to tempt me. And anon I took me to that our Lord had shewed me on the same day, with all the faith of Holy Church; for I beheld it as both in one, and fled thereto as to my comfort. And anon all vanished away, and I was brought to great rest and peace, without sickness of body, or dread of conscience.

The Sixty-eighth Chapter.

AND then our good Lord opened my ghostly eye, and shewed me my soul in the midst of my heart: I saw the soul so large as it were an endless world, and also as it were a blessed kingdom. And by the conditions that I saw therein, I understood that it is a worshipful city. In mids of that city our Lord Jesu very God and very man, a fair person and of large stature, highest Bishop, most solemne King, worshipful Lord. And I saw him clothed solemnly in worship; he sitteth in the soul, even right in peace and rest. And he ruleth and giveth heaven and earth, and all that is. The man-hood with the God-head sitteth in rest: the God-head ruleth and giveth without any instrument or business. And the soul is all occupied with the blessed Godhead; that is, sovereign might, sovereign wisdom, and severeign goodness. The place that Jesu taketh in our soul he shall never remove without end, as to my sight: for in us is his homliest home, and his endless dwelling. And in this he sheweth the liking that he hath of the making of mans soul; for as well as the Father might make a creature, and as well as the Son might make a creature so well would the Holy Ghost that mans soul were made, and so it was done. And therefore the blessedful Trinity enjoyeth without end in the making of mans soul: for he saw without beginning, what should like him without end. All thing that he hath made sheweth his Lordship, as understanding was given in the same time by example of a creature, that is led to see great nobleness, and kingdoms longing to a Lord. And when it had seen all the nobleness beneath, then marvelling, it was stirred to seek up above to that high place where the Lord dwelleth; knowing by reason that his dwelling is in the worthiest place. And thus I understand truly that our soul may never have rest in things that is beneath it self. And when it cometh above all creatures into it self, yet may it not abide in the beholding of it self; but all the beholding is blessedfully set in God; that is, the Maker dwelling therein; for in mans soul is his very dwelling. And the highest light and the brightest shining of the city is the glorious love of our Lord God, as to my sight. And what may make us more enjoy in God, than to see in him that he enjoyeth in us highest of all his works? For I saw in the same shewing that if the blessed Trinity might have made mans soul any better, any fairer, any nobler than it was made, he should not have been full pleased with making of mans soul: but for he made mans soul as fair, as good, as precious, as he might make it a creature, therefore the blessed Trinity is full pleased without end in the making of mans soul. And he will that our hearts be mightily raised above the deepness of the earth, and all vain sorrowes, and enjoy in him. This was a delectable sight, and a restful shewing that is without end: and the beholding of this whiles we are here, it is full pleasant to God, and full great speed to us. And the soul that thus beholdeth, it maketh him like to him that is beholden, and oned it in rest and in peace by his grace. And this was a singular joy and bliss to me that I saw him sitting: for the truth of sitting shewed endless dwelling. And he gave me knowing truly that it was he that shewed me all before: and when I had beholden all this with advisement; then shewed our good Lords words full meekly, without voice, and without opening of lips, right as he had done afore, and said full sweetly; '*Wit it now well, it was no raving that thou sawest to day: but take it and believe it, and keep thee therein, and comfort thee therewith, and trust thereto, and thou shalt not be overcome.'* These last words were said for learning of full true sikerness; that is, our Lord Jesu that shewed me all. And right as in the first word, that our good Lord shewed, meaning his blessed passion, '*herewith is the fiend overcome;*' right so he said in the last word, with full true faithfulness meaning us all: '*Thou shalt not be overcome.*' And all this learning and this true comfort is general to all mine even Christen, as it is aforesaid; and so is Gods will. And this word, '*Thou shalt not be overcome,*' was said full sharply, and full mightily for sickness and comfort against all tribulations that may come: he said not, thou shalt not be troubled, thou shalt not be travelled, thou shalt not be diseased; but he said, '*Thou shalt not be overcome.*' God will that we take heed at this word, and that we be ever mighty in faithful trusting in weal and woe; for he loveth us, and liketh us: and so will he that we love him and like him, and mightily trust in him, and all shall be well: and soon all was close, and I saw no more after this.

The Sixty-ninth Chapter.

THE fiende came again with his heat, and with his stench, and made me full busie. The stench was so vile and so painful, and bodily heat also dreadful and travellous.

Also I heard a bodily talking, as it had been of two bodies: and both to my thinking talked at one time, as they had held a parliament, with great business. And all was soft whistering. And I understood not what they said. And all this was to stir me to dispair; as methought, seeming to me as they scorned bidding of beads, which are said boystously, with much failing of devout intending, and wise diligence, the which we owe to God in our prayer. And our good Lord God gave me grace mightily to trust in him, and to comfort my soul with bodily speech, as I should have done to another person that had been travelled; methought that business might not be likened to no bodily likeness.

The Seventieth Chapter.

My bodily eye I set in the same cross, there I had seen in comfort afore that time. My tongue with speech of Christs passion, and rehersing the faith of Holy Church, and my heart to fasten on God with all the trust and the might that I thought to my self meaning, 'Thou hast now great business to keep thee in the faith, for that thou shouldest not be taken of thine enemies. Wouldest thou now fro this time evermore be so busie to keep thee from sin, this were a good and a soveraign occupation.' For I thought faithfully, were I safe from sin, I were full safe from all the fiends in hell, and enemies of my soul. And thus he occupied me all that night, and on the morrow, till it was about prime day. And anon they were all gone and passed, and there left nothing but stink, and lasted still a while: and I scorned him. And thus was I delivered of him by the vertue of Christs passion; for therewith is the fiend overcome, as our Lord Jesu Christ said afore. In all this blessed shewing our good Lord gave understanding that the sight should pass. Which blessed shewing the faith keepeth with his own good will and his grace; for he left with me neither signe, ne token, whereby I might know it. But he left with me his own blessed word in true understanding, bidding me full mightily that I should believe it, and so I do; blessed mote he be. I believe that he is our Saviour that shewed it, and that it is in the faith that he shewed. And therefore I love it ever joying, and thereto I am bound by all his own meaning, with the next words that follow: '*Keep thee therein, and comfort thee therewith, and trust thereto.*' Thus I am beholding to keep it in my faith: for on the same day that it was shewed, what time the sight was passed, as a wretch I forsook it, and openly I said that I had raved. Then our Lord Jesu of his mercy would not let it perish, but he shewed it all again within my soul with more fulhead, with the blessed light of his precious love, saying these words full mightily and full meekly; '*Wit it now well, it was no raving that thou saw this day; as if he had said, for the sight was passed from thee, thou lost it, and could or might not keep it: But wit it now;*' that is to say, '*now thou seest it.*' This was said not only for the same time; but also to set thereupon the ground of my faith, where he saith anon following; '*But take it, and learn it, and keep thee therein, and comfort thee therewith, and trust thereto, and thou shalt not be overcome.*'

The Seventy-first Chapter.

IN these six words that followeth, where he saith, '*Take it;*' his meaning is to fasten it faithfully in our heart; for he will it dwell with us in faith into our lives end, and after in fulhead of joy, willing that we have ever faithful trust of his blessedful promises, knowing his goodness. For our faith is contraried in diverse manner, by our own blindness, and our ghostly enemies within and without. And therefore our precious Lover helpeth us with ghostly light, and true teaching, on diverse manner within and without, whereby that we may know him. And therefore in what manner that he teacheth us, he will that we perceive him wisely, receiving him sweetly, and keep us in him faithfully. For *above the faith* is no goodness kept in this life, as to my sight. And *beneath the faith* is no health of soul. But in the faith there will our Lord we keep us: for we have by his goodness and his own working to keep us in the faith. And by his sufferance through ghostly enmity we are assaid in the faith, and made mighty. For if our faith had not enmity, it should deserve no meed, as by the understanding that I have in our Lords meaning. Glad, and merry, and sweet, is the blessedful lovely chear of our Lord to our souls; for he beheld us ever living in love-longing. And he will our soul be in glad chear to him, to yield him his meed. And thus I hope with his grace he hath, and more shall draw the utter chear to the inner, and make us all at one with him, and each of us with other in true lasting joy that is Jesu. I have meaning of *three* manner of chears of our Lord: the *first* is chear of passion, as he shewed whiles he was with us in this life dying. And though this beholding be mourning and swemful, yet it is glad and merry; for he is God. The *second* manner of chear it is pitty, and ruth, and compassion: and this sheweth he to all his lovers, with sikerness of keeping that hath need to his mercy. The *third* is the blissedful chear as it shall be without end. And this was oftenest shewed, and longest continued. And thus in the time of our pain and our woe, he sheweth to us chear of his passion and his cross, helping us to bear it by his own blessed vertue. And in time of our sinning, he sheweth to us chear of ruth and pity, mightily keeping us, and defending against all our enemies. And these *two* be the common chears which he sheweth to us in this life, therewith medling the *third:* and that is his blessed chear like in party as it shall be in heaven; and that is by gracious touching of sweet lightning of ghostly life, whereby that we are kept in true faith, hope, and charity with contrition and devotion, and also with contemplation, and all manner of true joyes and sweet comforts. The blessedful chear of our Lord God worketh it in us by grace. But now me behooveth to tell in what manner that I saw sin deadly, in the creatures which should not die for sin, but live in the joy of God without end. I saw that *two* contraries should not be together in one steed. The most contrarious that are, is the highest bliss, and the deepest pain. The highest bliss that is, is to have God in clerity of endless light, him verily seeing, him sweetly feeling, him all peaceable having in fulhead of joy: and thus was the blessedful chear of our Lord God shewed in party. In which shewing I saw that sin was the most contrary, so far forth that as long as we be medled with any part of sin, we shall never see clearly the blessed chear of God. And the horriblier, and the grievouser that our sins be, the deeper are we for that time fro this blessed sight. And therefore it seemeth to us oftentimes as we were in peril of death, and in a party of hell, for the sorrow and the pain that sin is to us. And thus we are dead for the time fro the very sight of our blessedful life. But in all this I saw faithfully that we be not dead in the sight of God, ne he passeth never from us; but he shall never have his full bless in us till we have our full bless in him, verily seeing his fair blessedful chear, for we are ordained thereto in kind, and getten thereto by grace. Thus I saw how sin is deadly for a short time to the blessed creatures of endless life; and ever the more clearly that the soul seeth the blissful chear by grace of loving, the more it longeth to see it in fulhead; that is to say, in his own likeness: for notwithstanding that our Lord God dwelleth now in us, and is here with us, and colleth us, and becloseth us for tender love that he may never leave us, and is more near to us than tongue may tell, or heart may think: yet may we never stint of mourning, ne of weeping, nor of seeking, nor of longing, till when we see him clear in his blessedful chear: for in that precious sight there may no woe abide, nor weal fail. And in this I saw matter of mirth, and matter of mourning: matter of mirth, that our Lord our maker is so near to us, and in us, and we in him by faithfulness of keeping of his great goodness. Matter of mourning for our ghostly eye is so blind, and we so boarn down with weight of our deadly flesh, and darkness of sin, that we may not see our Lord God clearly in his blessedful chear; No, and because of this darkness, scarce we can believe or trowe his great love and our faithfulness of keeping. And therefore it is that I say, we may never leave off mourning, ne weeping: this weeping meaneth not all in pouring out of tears by our bodily eye, but also to more ghostly understanding; for the kindly desire of our soul is so great, and so unmeasurable, that if it were given us to our joy and our comfort, all the nobly that ever God made in heaven and in earth, and we saw not the fair blessedful chear of himself, yet should we never leave mourning ne of ghostly weeping; that is to say, of painful longing, till when we see verily the fair blessedful chear of our Maker. And if we were in all the pain that heart may think, or tongue may tell; and we might in that time see his blessedful chear, all this pain should us not grieve. Thus is that blessedful sight end of all manner of pain to loving souls, and fulfilling of all manner of joy and bliss. And that shewed he in the high marvellous words where he saith; '*I it am that is highest; I it am that thou lovest; I it am that is all.*' It longeth to us to have *three* manner of knowings. The *first* is, that we know our Lord God. The *second* is, that we know ourself; what we are by him in kind and in grace: the *third* is, that we know meekly that our self is against our sin and against our feebleness. And for these three was all this shewing made, as to my understanding.

The Seventy-second Chapter.

ALL this blessed teaching of our Lord God was shewed by *three* parts; that is to say, by bodily sight, and by word formed in my understanding, and by ghostly sight. For the bodily sight, I have said as I saw as truly as I can: and for the words, I have said them right as our Lord shewed them me: and for the ghostly sight, I have said some deal, but I may never full tell it. And therefore of this ghostly sight I am stirred to say more as God will give me grace. God shewed *two* manner of sickness that we have: that *one* is unpatience, or slouth; for we bear our travel and our pain heavily. That *other* is despair or doubtful dreed, as I shall say after: generally he shewed sin wherein all is comprehended, but in special he shewed none but these two. And these two are it that most travelleth and troubleth us, as by that our Lord shewed me. Of which he will we be amended; I speak of such men and women that for Gods love hate sin, and dispose them to do Gods will: then by our ghostly blind-head and bodily heaviness, we are most enclining to this. And therefore it is Gods will that they be known, and then should we refuse them, as we do other sins. And for help against this, full meekly our Lord shewed the patience that he had in this hard passion: and also the joy and the liking that he hath of that passion for love. And this he shewed in example, that we should gladly and easily bear our pains; for that is great pleasing to him, and endless profit to us. And the cause why we are travelled with them is for unknowing of love. Though the Three Persons of the blessed Trinity be all even in the self: the soul took most understanding in love; yea, and he will in all thing that we have our beholding and our enjoying in love. And of this knowing are we most blind. For some of us believe that God is all mighty, and may do all; and that he is all wisdom, and can do all: but that he is all love and will do all, there we fail. And this unknowing it is that most letteth Gods lovers, as to my sight: for when we begin to hate sin, and amend us by the ordinance of Holy Church, yet there dwelleth a dread that letteth us, by the beholding of our self and of our sin afore done. And some of us for our every day sins, for we hold not our promise, nor keep our cleanness that our Lord setteth us in, but fall oft-times into so much wretchedness, that shame it is to say it. And the beholding of this maketh us so sorry, and so heavy, that unneths we can see any comfort. And this dread we take sometime for a meekness, but it is a foul blindness, and a wickedness. And we cannot despise it as we do another sin that we know, which cometh through lack of true judgment, and it is again truth: for of all the properties of the blissedful Trinity it is Gods will that we have most faithfulness and liking in love; for love maketh might and wisdom full meek to us. For right as by the courtesie of God he forgetteth our sin after the time that we repent us: so will he that we forget our sin as against our unskillful heaviness, and our doubtful dreads.

The Seventy-third Chapter.

For I understood *four* manner of dreads: *one* is dread of a fray that cometh to man suddenly by frailty. This dread doth good, for it helpeth to purge man, as doth bodily sickness, or such other pain that is not sin; for all such pains help man, if they be patiently taken. The *second* is dread of pain; whereby man is stirred and waked fro sleep of sin: for man that is hard of sleep of sin, he is not able for the time to receive the soft comfort of the Holy Ghost, till he hath undertaken this dread of pain, of bodily death and of ghostly enemies. And this dread stirreth us to seek comfort and mercy of God. And thus this dread helpeth us as an entry, and ableth us to have contrition by the blissedful touching of the Holy Ghost. The *third* is doubtful dread: doubtful dread is as much as it draweth to despair; God will have it turned in us into love, by true knowing of love; that is to say, that the bitterness of doubts be turned into sweetness of kind love by grace; for it may never please our Lord that his servants doubt in his goodness. The *fourth* is reverent dread; for there is no dread that fully pleaseth God in us, but reverent dread, and that is soft. For the more it is had, the less it is felt for sweetness of love. Love and dread are brethren, and they are rooted in us by the goodness of our Maker, and they shall never be taken from us without end. We have of kind to love, and we have of grace to love; and have we of kind to dread, and we have of grace to dread. It longeth to the lordship, and to the father-head to be dread, as it longeth to the goodness to be loved: and it longeth to us that are his servants and his children to dread him for lordship, and fatherhead; as it longeth to us to love him for God-head. And though this reverent dread and love be not both in one, but are two in property and in working, and neither of them may be had without other. And therefore I am sure, he that loveth he dreadeth, though he feel it but little. All dreads other than reverend dread that are proferred to us, though they come under colour of holiness, they are not so true. And hereby may they be known asunder. That dread that maketh us hastily to flee fro all that is not good, and fall into our Lords breast; as the child into the mothers arme, with all our intent, and with all our mind, knowing our feebleness and our great need, knowing his everlasting goodness and his blessed love, only seeking into him for salvation, cleaving to with faithful trust: that dread that bringeth us into this working, it is kind and gracious, and good, and true. And all that is contrarious to this, either it is wrong, or it is medled with wrong. Then is this the remedy to know them both, and refuse the wrong: for the kind property of dread which we have in this life by the gracious working of the Holy Ghost, the same shall be in heaven afore God, gentle, courteous, full sweet. And thus we shall in love be homely and near to God. And we in dread be gentle and curteous to God, and both in one manner like even. Desire we then of our Lord God to dread him reverently, and love him meekly, and to trust in him mightily: for when we dread him reverently, and love him meekly, our trust is never in vain; for the more that we trust, and the mightilier that we trust, the more we please and worship our Lord that we trust in. And if us fail this reverent dread and meek love, as God forbid we should, our trust shall soon be mis-ruled for that time. And therefore us needeth much to pray our Lord of grace that we may have this reverent dread, and make love of his gift in heart and in work, for without this no man may please God.

The Seventy-fourth Chapter.

I SAW that God may do all that us deedeth: and these three that I shall say, need, love, longing: pitty and love keepeth us in the time of our need. And longing in the same love draweth us into heaven; for the thirst of God is to have the general man into him. In which thirst he hath drawn his holy souls that be now in bliss. And so getting his lively members, ever he draweth and drinketh, and yet him thirsteth and longeth. I saw *three* manner of longings in God, and all to one end. The *first* is, for that he longeth to learn us to know him and to love him ever more and more, as it is convenient and speedful to us. The *second* is, that he longeth to have us up into bliss, as souls are when they be taken out of pain into heaven. The *third* is, to fulfill us of bliss, and that shall be on the last day fulfilled ever to last. For I saw, as it is known in our faith, that then pain and sorrow shall be ended to all that shall be saved. And not only we shall receive the same bliss that souls afore have had in heaven, but also we shall receive a new, which plentuously shall flie out of God into us, and fulfill us. And those be the goods which he hath ordained to give us fro without beginning. These goods are treasured and hid in himself; for into that time creature is not mighty, ne worthy to receive them. In this we should see verily the cause of all the deeds that God hath done. And over-more we should see the cause of all thing that he hath suffered: and the bliss, and the fulfilling shall be so deep and so high, that for wonder and marvel all creatures should have to God so great reverent and dread over-passing, that hath been seen and felt before that the pillars of heaven shall travel and quake. But this manner of trembling and dread shall have no manner of pain; but it longeth to the worthy majesty of God, thus to be beholden of his creatures dreadfully trembling and quaking: for much more of joy endlesly marvelling of the greatness of God the Maker, and of the least part of all that is made. For the beholding of this maketh creature marvellous meek and mild. Wherefore God will, and also it longeth to us both in kind and in grace, to will to have knowing of this desiring the sight and the working. For it leadeth us in right way, and keepeth us in true life, and oneth us to God. And as good as God is, as great he is: and as much as it longeth to his God-head to be loved, so much it longeth to his great highness to be dread. For this reverent dread is the fairer courtesie that is in heaven before Gods face. And as much as he shall be known and loved, over-passing that he is now: in so much he shall be dread over-passing that he is now. Wherefore it behooveth needs to be, that all heaven, all earth shall tremble and quake when the pillars shall tremble and quake.

The Seventy-fifth Chapter.

I SPEAK but little of this reverent dread: for I hope it may be seen in this matter aforesaid. But well I wote that our Lord shewed me no souls but those that dread him; for well I wote the soul that truly taketh the teaching of the Holy Ghost, it hateth more sin for the vileness and the horribility, than it doth all the pain that is in hell. For the soul that beholdeth the kindness of our Lord Jesu, it hateth no hell; but hell is sin as to my sight. And therefore it is Gods will that we know sin, and pray busily, and travel wilfully, and seek teaching meekly, that we fall not blindly therein; and if we fall, that we rise readily: for it is the most pain that the soul may have to turn from God any time by sin. The soul that will be in rest when other mens sins come to mind, he should flee it as the pain of hell, seeking into God for help again that, for the beholding of other mens sin, it maketh as it were a thick mist afore the eye of the soul. And we may not for the time see the fair-head of God, but if we may behold them with contrition with him, with compassion on him, and with holy desire to God for him. For without this it noieth, and troubleth, and letteth the soul that behold them; for this I understand in the shewing of the compassion. In this blessedful shewing of our Lord I have understanding of *two* contrarious. *That one* is the most wisdom that any creature may do in this life. *That other* is the most folly. The most wisdom is a creature to do after the will and the counsel of his highest sovereign friend. This blessed friend is Jesu, and it is his will and counsel that we hold us with him, and fasten us homely to him, evermore in what state soever we bene: for whether we be foul or clean, we are ever one in his loving. For weal, ne for woe he will never we flee him; but for the change-ability that we are in our self, we fall often into sin; than have we this by the stirring of our enemy, and by our own folly and blindness: for they say thus, "Thou wotest well thou art a wretch, a sinner, and also untrue, for thou keepest not thy covenant. Thou promisest oftentimes our Lord that thou shalt do better; and anon thou fallest again in the same, namely in slouth, and leesing of time." For that is the beginning of sin as to my sight; and namely, to the creatures that have given themself to serve our Lord with inward beholding of his blessedful goodness. And this maketh us adread to appear afore our courteous Lord. Than is it our enemy that will put us a back with his false dread of our wretchedness, for pain that he threateth us by, for it is his meaning to make us so heavy and so sorry in this, that we should let out of mind the blessedful beholding of our everlasting friend.

The Seventy-sixth Chapter.

Our good Lord shewed the enmity of the fiend, whereby I understood that all that is contrarious to love and to peace, it is of the fiend, and of his party; and we have of our feebleness and our folly to fall: and we have of mercy and of grace of the Holy Ghost to rise to more joy. And if our enemy ought winneth of us by our falling (for it is his likeness) he leeseth many times more in our rising by charity and meekness. And this glorious rising it is so great sorrow and pain to him, for the hate that he hath to our soul, that he brenneth continually in envy. And all this sorrow that he would make us to have, it shall turn into himself. And for this it was that our Lord scorned him, and shewed that he shall be scorned; and this made me mightily to laugh. Then is this the remedy that we be a known of our wretchedness, and flie to our Lord: for ever the more needier that we be, the more speedful it is to us to touch him; and say we thus in our meaning; 'I know well that I have deserved pain, but our Lord is Almighty, and may punish me mightily; and he is all wisdom, and can punish me wisely, and he is all goodness, and loveth me tenderly.' And in this beholding it is speedful to us to abide; for it is a full lovely meekness of a sinful soul wrought by mercy and grace of the Holy Ghost: when we will wilfully and gladly take the scourging and the chastising that our Lord himself will give us, and it shall be full tender and full easie if we will only hold us pleased with him, and with all his works. For that penance that man taketh upon himself, it was not shewed me; that is to say, it was not shewed me specified; but this was shewed specially, and highly, and with full lovely chear, that we should meekly and patiently bear and suffer that penance that God himself giveth us, with mind of his blessed passion; for when we have mind of his blessed passion with pitty and love: then we suffer with him, like as his friends did that saw it. And this was shewed in the xiiith. neer at the beginning, where it speaketh of pity; for he saith, '*Accuse not thy self that thy tribulation and thy woe is all thy default: for I will not that thou be heavy, ne sorrowful undiscreetly; for I tell thee, howsoever thou do thou shalt have woe. And therefore I will that thou wisely know thy penance which thou art in continually, and that thou meekly take it for thy penance. And then shalt thou truly see that all this living is penance profitable.*' This place is prison; this life is penance, and in the remedy he will that we enjoy. The remedy is, that our Lord is with us, keeping us, and leading into fulhead of joy; for this is an endless joy to us in our Lords meaning; that he that shall be our bliss when we are there, he is our Keeper while we are here; our way and our heaven, in true love and faithful trust. And of this he gave understanding in all, and namely, in shewing of his passion, where he made me mightily to choose him for my heaven. Flee we to our Lord, and we shall be comforted, touch we him, and we shall be made clean; cleave we to him, and we shall be sure and safe from all manner of perils; for our courteous Lord will that we be as homely with him, as heart may think, or soul may desire. But be we ware that we take not so retchesly this homely-head for to leave courtesie; for our Lord himself is sovereign homely-head, and so homely as he is, as courteous he is; for he is very courteous. And the blessed creatures that shall be in heaven with him without end, he will have them like to himself in all thing; and to be like to our Lord perfectly, it is our very salvation and our full bliss. And if we wote not how we shall do, all this, desire we of our Lord, and he shall learn us; for it is his own liking and his worship: blessed mote he be.

The Seventy-seventh Chapter.

Our Lord of his mercy sheweth us our sin and our feebleness by the sweet gracious sight of himself. For our sin is so foul and so horrible, that he of his curtesie will not shew it us but by the light of his mercy. Of *four* things, it is his will that we have knowing: the *first* is, that he is the ground of whom we have all our life and our being. The *second* is, that he keepeth us mightily and mercifully in the time that we are in our sin, among all our enemies that are full fell upon us. And somuch we are in the more peril, for we give them occasion thereto, and we know not our own need. The *third* is, how curteously he keepeth us, and maketh us to know that we go amiss. The *fourth* is, how stedfastly he abideth us, and changeth no chear; for he will that we be turned and unied to him in love, as he is to us. And thus by gracious knowing we may see our sin profitable without despair: for soothly us needeth to see it; and by the sight we should be made ashamed of our self, and breaking down as against our pride and our presumption: for us behooveth verily to see that of our self we are right naught but sin and wretchedness. And thus by the sight of the less *(part of sin)* that our Lord sheweth us, the more is wasted, which we see not: for he of his courtesie measureth the sight to us: for it is so foul and so horrible, that we should not endure to see it as it is. And thus by this meek knowing through contrition and grace we shall be broken from all thing that is not our Lord. And then shall our blessed Saviour perfectly cure us, and one us to him. This breaking, and this curing our Lord meaneth by the general man; for he that is highest and nearest with God, he may see himself sinful and needy with me. And I that am the least and the lowest of those that shall be saved; I may be comforted with him that is highest: so hath our Lord oned us in charity, when he shewed me that I should sin. And for joy that I had in beholding him, I entended not readily to that shewing. And our courteous Lord rested there, and would no further teach me, till when that he gave me grace and will to entend. And hereof was I learned, though that we be highly lifted into contemplation by the special gift of our Lord, yet us behooveth needs therewith to have sight and knowing of our sin, and of our feebleness. For without this knowing we may not have true meekness; and without this we may not be safe. And also I saw we may not have this knowing of our self, nor of none of all our ghostly enemies; for they will not us so much good: for if it were by their will, we should never see it till our ending day. Then are we much bound to God that he will himself for love shew it us in time of mercy and grace.

The Seventy-eighth Chapter.

Also I had in this more understanding, in that he shewed me that I should sin. I took it nakedly to my own singular person for I was no otherwise stirred in that time: but by the high gracious comfort that followed after I saw, that his meaning was for the general man; that is to say, all man which is sinful, and shall be into the last day: of which man I am a member as I hope by the mercy of God; for the blessed comfort that I saw, it is large enough for us all. And there was I learned that I should see mine own sin, and not other mens, but if it may be for comfort or help of my even Christen. And also in the same shewing, there I saw that I should sin:

there was I learned to be dreadful for unsikerness of my self. For I wot not how I shall fall, ne I know not the measure, ne the greatness of my sin: for that would I a wist dreadful; and thereto I had none answer. Also our courteous Lord in that same time, he shewed full sweetly and full mightily the endless-head, and the unchangeability of his love: and also his great goodness, and his gracious inwardly keeping, that the love of him and of our souls shall never be departed into without end. And thus in the dread I have matter of meekness, that saveth me fro presumption. And in the blessed shewing of love I have matter of true comfort and of joy, that saveth me from despair. All this homely shewing of our courteous Lord it is a lovely lesson, and a sweet gracious teaching of himself in comforting of our soul: for he will that we know by the sweetness of the homely love of him, that all that we see or feel within or without, which is contrarious to this, that it is of the enemy, and not of God; as thus, if that we be stirred to be the more retchlesser of our living, or of the keeping of our heart, because that we have knowing of this plentuous love; than needeth us greatly to beware of this stirring, if it come. It is untrue, and greatly we owe to hate it, for it hath no likeness of Gods will; and when befallen by frailty or blindness. Then our courteous Lord touching us, stirreth us and keepeth. And then will he that we see our wretchedness, and meekly be it a known. But he will not that we abide therewith, ne he will not that we busie us greatly about our accusing, ne he will not that we be too wretchedful on our self; but he will that we hastily entend to him: for he standeth all alone, and abideth us continually, moaning and mourning till when we come. And he hath haste to have us to him: for we are his joy and his delight, and he is our salve of our life; there I say he standeth all alone. I leave the speaking of the blessed company in heaven, and speak only of his office and his working here in earth, upon the condition of the shewing.

The Seventy-ninth Chapter.

BY *three* things man standeth in this life: by which three God is worshipped, and we be speed, kept, and saved. The *first* is, use of mans kindly reason. The *second* is, the common teaching of Holy Church. The *third* is, the inward gracious working of the Holy Ghost. And these *three* be all of one God. God is ground of our kindly reason; and God is teaching of Holy Church; and God is the Holy Ghost. And all be sundry gifts to which he will we have great regard, and according us thereto: for these work in us continually altogether, and those be great things. Of which greatness he will we have knowing here as it were in an A. B. C. that is to say, that we may have a little knowing, whereof we should have fulhead in heaven: and that is for to speed us. We know in our faith that God alone took our kind, and none but hee: and furthermore, that Christ alone did all the great works that longeth to our salvation, and none but he: and right so he alone doth now in the last end; that is to say, he dwelleth here in us, and ruleth us, and giveth us in this living, and bringeth us to his bliss. And thus shall he do as long as any soul is in earth that shall come to heaven: and so far forth, that if there were none such soul in earth but one, he should be with that all alone, till he had brought it up to his bliss. I believe and understand the ministration of holy angels as clarkes tell; but it was not shewed me: for himself is nearest and meekest, highest and lowest, and doth all. And not only all that us needeth, but also he doth all that is worshipful to our joy in heaven. And there I say he abideth us moaning and mourning. It meaneth all the true feeling that we have in our self in contrition and in compassion; and all moaning and mourning, for we are not oned with our Lord, and such as is speedful it is Christ in us. And though some of us feel it seldom, it passeth never fro Christ, till what time he have brought us out of all our woe: for love suffereth him never to be without pity. And what time that we fall into sin, and leave the mind of him, and the keeping of our own soul, then beareth Christ alone all the charge of us. And thus standeth he moaning and mourning. Then longeth it to us for reverence and kindness to turn us hastily to our Lord, and let him not all alone; he is here alone with us all; that is to say, only for us he is here. And what time I be strange to him by sin, despair, or slouth, then I let my Lord stand alone, in as much as he is in me. And thus it fareth with us all which be sinners. But though it be so that we do thus oftentimes, his goodness suffereth us never to be alone, but lastingly he is with us, and tenderly he excuseth us, and ever keepeth us from blame in his sight.

The Eightieth Chapter.

OUR good Lord shewed him to his creature in diverse manner, both in heaven and in earth. But I saw him take no place, but in mans soul. He shewed him in earth in the sweet incarnation, and his blessed passion, and in other manner he shewed him in earth, where I said I saw God in a point. And in other manner he shewed him in earth, thus as it were a pilgrimage; that is to say, he is here with us leading us, and shall be till when he hath brought us all to his bliss in heaven. He shewed him diverse times raigning, as it is aforesaid; but principally in mans soul: he hath taken there his resting place, and his worshipful city; out of which worshipful see he shall never rise, ne remove without end. Marvellous and solemn is the place where the Lord dwelleth. And therefore he will that we readily entend to his gracious touching, more enjoying in his whole love, then sorrowing in our often fallings. For it is the most worship to him of any thing, that we may do, that we live gladly and merrily for his love in our penance; for he beholdeth us so tenderly, that he seeth all our living here to be penance. For kind longing in us to him is a lasting penance in us, which penance he worketh in us, and mercifully helpeth us to bear it; for his love maketh him to long: his wisdom and his truth with his rightful-head maketh him to suffer us here. And in this manner he will see it in us; for this is our kindly penance, and the highest to my sight. For this penance cometh never fro us, till what time that we be fulfilled, when we should have him to our meed. And therefore he will that we set our hearts in the over-passing; that is to say, fro the pain that we feel into the bliss that we trust.

The Eighty-first Chapter.

But here shewed our courteous Lord the moaning and the mourning of our soul, meaning thus: '*I wot well thou wilt live for my love, merrily and gladly suffering all the penance that may come to thee: but forasmuch as thou livest not without sin, therefore thou art heavy and sorrowful. And if thou mightest live without sin, thou wouldest suffer for my love all the woe that might come to thee, and it is sooth: but be not too much agrieved with sin that falleth to thee against thy will,' (that is; not maliciously.)* And here I understood that the Lord beheld the servant with pity, and not with blaim; for this passing life asketh not to live all without sin. He loveth us endlesly, and we sin customably; and he sheweth it us full mildely, and then we sorrow and mourn discreetly, turning us into the beholding of his mercy, cleaving to his love and to his goodness, seeing that he is our medicine, witting that we do *(nothing)* but sin. And thus by the meekness that we get in the sight of our sin, faithfully knowing his everlasting love, him thanking and praising, we please him. '*I love thee and thou lovest me, and our love shall never be departed on two; and for thy profit I suffer.*' And all this was shewed in ghostly understanding, saying this blessed word; '*I keep thee full sikerly.*' And by the great desire that I saw in our blessed Lord, that we should live in this manner; that is to say, in longing and enjoying, as all this lesson of love sheweth. Thereby I understand that all that is contrarious to this, it is not of him, but it is of enmity. And he will that we know it by the sweet gracious light of his kind love. If any such liver be in earth which is continually kept from falling, I know it not; for it was not shewed me. But this was shewed, that in falling, and in rising we are ever preciously kept in one love, *(by which we were chosen before others from all eternity.)* For in the beholding of God we fall not. And in the beholding of our self, we stand not. And both these be sooth, as to my sight. But the beholding of our Lord God is the higher soothness. Then are we much bound to him, that he will in this living shew us this high soothness. And I understood whiles we be in this life, it is full speedful to us that we see these both at once. For the higher beholding keepeth us in ghostly joy, and true enjoying in God: that other that is the lower beholding, keepeth us in dread, and maketh us ashamed of ourself. But our good Lord will ever that we hold us much more in the beholding of the higher, and not leave the knowing of the lower into the time that we be brought up above, where we shall have our Lord Jesu to our meed, and be fulfilled of joy and bliss without end.

The Eighty-second Chapter.

I HAD in party touching, sight, and feeling in *three* properties of God, in which the strength and the effect of all the revelation standeth. And it were seen in every shewing: and most properly in the twelfth, where it saith oftentimes, '*I it am.*' The properties are these, life, love, and light. In life is marvellous homelihead. In love is gentle courtesie: and in light is endless kindness. These *three* properties were seen in one goodness; into which goodness my reason would be oned and cleaving to with all the mights. I beheld with reverent dread, and highly marvelling in the sight and in feeling of the sweet accord that our reason is in God, understanding that it is the highest gift that we have received, and it is grounded in kind. Our faith is a light kindly coming of our endless day; that is our Father God: in which light our mother Christ, and our good Lord the Holy Ghost leadeth us in this passing life. This light is measured discreetly, needfully standeth to us in the night; the light is cause of our life; the night is cause of our pain, and all our woe: in which woe we desire endless meed and thank of God, for we with mercy and grace wilfully know and believe our light, going therein wisely and mightily. And at the end of woe suddenly our eye shall be opened, and in clearness of sight our light shall be full: which light is God our Maker, Father and Holy Ghost, in Christ Jesu our Saviour. Thus I saw and understood that our faith is our light, in our night, which light is God our endless day.

The Eighty-third Chapter.

THIS light is charity, and the measuring of this light is done to us profitably by the wisdom of God: for neither the light is so large that we may see clearly our blessedful day: ne it is all speered from us; but it is such a light in which we may live meedfully with travel, reserving the worshipful thanks of God. And this was seen in the vi*th* shewing, where he saith, '*I thank thee of thy service, and of thy travel.*' Thus charity keepeth us in faith, and in hope: and faith and hope leadeth us in charity; and at the end all shall be charity. I had *three* manner of understandings in this light of charity: the *first* is charity unmade: the *second* is charity made: the *third* is charity given. Charity unmade is God; charity made is our soul in God: charity given is vertue, and that is a gracious gift of working; in which we love God for himself, and our self in God, and all that God loveth for God.

The Eighty-fourth Chapter.

AND in this sight I marvelled highly; for notwithstanding our simple living, and our blindness here, yet endlesly our courteous Lord beholdeth us in this working, enjoying. And of all thing we may please him best, wisely and truly to believe it, and to enjoy with him and in him; for as verily as we shall be in bliss of God without end, him praising and thanking, as verily we have been in the foresight of God, loved and known in his endless purpose fro without beginning. In which unbegun love he made us; in the same love he keepeth us, and never suffereth us to be hurt, by which our bliss might be lessed. And therefore when the doome is given, and we be all brought up above, then shall we clearly see in God the privities which now be hid to us. And then shall none of us be stirred to say in any thing, 'Lord, if it had been thus, it had been well.' But we shall all say with one voyce, 'Lord, blessed mote thou be, for it is thus: thus it is well. And now we see verily, that all thing is done as it was thine ordinance or any thing was made.'

The Eighty-fifth Chapter.

This book is begun by Gods gift and his grace; but it is not yet performed as to my sight. For charity pray we all together, with Gods working, thanking, trusting, enjoying. For this will our good Lord be praid, by the understanding that I took in all his own meaning. And in the sweet words where he saith full merrily, '*I am ground of thy beseeching.*' For truly, I saw and understood in our Lords meaning, that he shewed it; for he will have it knowing more then it is. In which knowing he will give us grace to love him, and cleave to him. For he beholds his heavenly treasure and solace in heavenly joy, in drawing of our hearts from sorrow and darkness, which we are in. And fro the time that it was shewed, I desired oftentimes to wit in what was our Lords meaning: and fifteen year after and more, I was answered in ghostly understanding, saying thus; '*What? wouldest thou wit thy Lords meaning in this thing? Wit it well: love was his meaning. Who sheweth it thee? Love. Wherefore sheweth he it thee? For love. Hold thee therein, thou shalt wit more in the same. But thou shalt never wit therein other without end.*' Thus was I learned that love is our Lords meaning. And I saw full surely in this and in all that our God made us, he loved us; which love was never slacked, ne never shall. And in this love he hath done all his works: and in this love he hath made all thing profitable to us: and in this love our life is everlasting; in our making we had beginning: but the love wherein he made us was in him fro without beginning. In which love we have our beginning. And all this shall we see in God without end.

Deo Gratias.

Explicit liber Revelationum Juliane Anachorite Norwic. cujus anime propicietur Deus.

THE END.

GLOSSARY.

A.

A. B. C, *elements of learning.* 'Of which greatness he will we have knowing here as it were in an A. B. C.'

Abide, *to wait for, tarry.*

Abiden, *waited for.*

Abidings, *tarryings for.*

Able, *to enable, help.*

Abode, *waited.*

Accord, *to harmonize, join, to agree.*

Accord, *harmony, agreement.*

Adred, *afraid.*

Adventure, *contingency.*

Advice, or Advise, *consideration, attention, circumspection.*

Advisement, *or* Avisement, *same as* Advice.

After as, *or* After that, *accordingly as.*

Again, *against.*

Again-being, *redemption.*

All, *altogether.*

All to, *entirely.* All to breaketh: *entirely breaketh.*

Anaved? 'It seemed that he was anaved; that is to say, new beginning for to travel.'

Aneynst, Anent, Anenst, Aneinst, *or* Anempts, *opposite, over against, with, according to, touching.*

And, *if.*

Anon, *presently, immediately.*

Appay, *to satisfy, recompense.*

Apaid, *content, satisfied.*

Arraid, *arrayed.*

As, *all so, omnino sic.*

Assaid, *tried, tested.*

Assay, *or* Assey, *trial, test.*

Asseethe, *satisfaction.*

Asseeth-making, *making satisfaction.*

Assoon, *immediately.*

B.

Be, *been.*

Be-christened. 'Whether they have be-christened or not.'

Beclipping, *embracing.*

Beclose, *to enclose, shut in.*

Becometh, *cometh.*

Begrowing, *growing, increasing.*

Behaviour, *appearance.* 'And the shape at his outward behaviour.' Shakespear uses it in the sense of an assumed character:

> "Thus, after greeting, speaks the king of France,
> In my behaviour, to the Majesty,
> The borrow'd Majesty of England here."
>
> JOHN i. 1.

Behest, *promise.*

Behighting, *assurance, promise.*

Beholden, *beheld.*

Beholding, *beholden.*

Behove, *to be fit, meet, necessary.*

Behovely, *necessary, behoveful.*

Been, *or* Bene, *be.*

Belongen, *belong, or belonged.*

Bene, *been.*

Benedicite, *an exclamation answering to our Bless us!* Benedicite Dominus.

Beseek, *to beseech.*

Beseekinge, *beseeching, desire, entreaty.*

Besides, *on the sides.* 'For besides, the cross was no sureness for dreed of fiends.'

Bidding of beads, *prayer.*

Black-head, *blackness.*

Blaim, *blame.*

Blesse, *blessing, bliss?* 'And loving of God in the blesse of heaven.'

Blessedful *or* Blissedful, *full of blessedness or bliss.*

Blessedfully, *in a way full of blessedness.*

Bless-ful, *full of blessing.*

Blew-head, *blueness.*

Blind-head, *blindness.*

Bliveth, *abideth, remaineth.*

Blood-shed, *bleeding.*

Boarn, *borne.*

Boystrous, *hasty, rough.*

Boystously, *hastily, roughly.*

Breaking, *broken.*

Brenneth, *burneth.*

Brent, *burnt.*

Briken, *broken.*

Broad, *wide.*

Brown-head, *brown colour.*

Brows, *forehead.*

Bulke, *body.*

Business, *toil, engrossing occupation.* 'The Godhead ruleth and giveth without any instrument or business.'

But, (adv.) *only, unless.*

But, (prep.) *without.*

But if, *unless.*

But that, *otherwise than, except.*

Buxom, *compliant, lowly, obedient.*

Buxomness, *kindness, inclination.*

Buying, *redeeming.*

C.

Charge, *load, burthen.*

Charity, *love.*

Chere, Cheer, *or* Chear, *countenance, appearance, entertainment.*

Childhead, *or* Childhood, *state or condition of a child.*

Christen, *Christian.*

Christendome, *baptism.*

Clark, *a person in holy orders, a man of learning.*

Clerity, *clearness, glory.*

Clinging, *withering.*

Cloggering, *sticking together, adhering, coalescing.*

Clongen, *withered.*

Close, *closed.*

Close, (adv.) *secretly.*

Clottered, *clotted.*

Colleth, *embraceth.*

Common, *as opposed to special and privy.*

Common *or* Commune, *community.* 'With all the blessed common:' *communion of saints.*

Commoning, *communing.*

Compassion, *fellow-suffering.*

Condition, *manner, state of things.* 'With a condition:' *with limitation or reserve.*

Continuant, *continual.*

Contrarie, *to contradict.*

Contraried, *opposed.*

Contrarious, *opposite, opposed, perverse.*

Contrariousness, *opposition, perversity.*

Conveniable, *convenient, suitable, proper.*

Could, *cold.* 'It was a dry sharp wind, wonder could, as to my sight.'

Courteous, *or* Curteous, *condescending, complaisant.*

Courtesiest, *most courteous.*

Cure, *care.*

Customably, *as a matter of custom, according to custom.*

D.

Daliance, *interchange of love.*

Deadlie, *mortal, devoted to death.*

Deale, *a part?* 'Some deale.'

Debt, *duties.*

Deedeth, *doeth?* 'I saw that God may do all that us deedeth:' *perhaps a misprint for* needeth.

Deem, *to judge.*

Deeming, *judgement or estimation of things, opinion.*

Default, *want, defect.*

Defaulted, *defective.*

Defaulting, *defectiveness.*

Delectable, *delightful.*

Delve, *to dig.*

Depart, *to separate, divide, to be separate.*

Departing, *separation, difference.*

Descrie, *to discern, discover.*

Despite, *malice, anger, hatred, defiance.*

Despiteous, *malicious, angry to excess.*

Dight, *a disposing, ordering, appointment.*

Dight, *to prepare, appoint, dress, adorn, appropriate.*

Diking, *ditching.*

Direct, *plain, express.*

Disease, *want of ease, pain.*

Disease, *to give pain.*

Dissolation, *misery.*

Domes-man, *judge, confessor.*

Done, *an old form of,* to do. 'So will he that we done as the meek child.'

Doom, *judgment, sentence.*

Doomsday, *judgment-day.*

Door, *doer.* 'For there is no Door but he.'

Dread, *to fear, stand in awe of, reverence.*

Dread, *dreaded.* 'It longeth to his great highness to be dread.'

Dread, *or* Dreed, *fear, doubt, awe, reverence.*

Dreadful, *awful, fearful, to be feared, timorous, reverential.*

Dreadfully, *in awe or fear.*

Dure, *endure.*

Duringly, *enduringly.*

Dwelling, *delay? sojourn.*

E.

Each, *every.*

Earnest, *zeal, studious pursuit of any thing, pledge.*

Eien, *or* Eyen, *eyes.*

Endeles, *endless.*

Endleslie, *endlessly.*

Endlesse-head, *endlessness.*

Enformed, *informed.*

Entend, *to attend.*

Entent, *intent.*

Entry, *entrance, commencement.*

Even, *fellow, equal.* 'Even christen:' *fellow christian.*

Even forth, *straight forward.*

Evenly, *equally.*

Every, *ever?* 'That we meekly suffer, every enjoying in God.'

Evesing, *eaves.*

F.

Fair, *beauteous.*

Fair-head, *beauty, fairness.*

Father-head, *or* Fatherhood, *state or condition of a father, all which appertains to a father.*

Faulting, *wanting, failing.*

Feeled, *felt.*

Feeling, *sense, perception.*

Fell, *cruel, destructive.*

Find, *to supply.* 'Wherefore him behoveth to find us, for the dear worthy love of motherhood hath made him debtor to us.'

Flaming, *flying abroad.*

Followen, *follow, or followed.*

For, *because, because that.*

Force, 'give no force:' *cared not.*

Fordreth, *nourisheth.*

Fore, *before.*

Foresaid, *or* Aforesaid, 'In his endless foresaid purpose.'

Forget, *forgotten?* 'It is Gods will that we know he hath not forget us.'

Forth, *forward.* As far forth, Forthwithall, So far forth.

Forth-bringing, *birth.*

Forth-speeding, *increase of profiting.*

Forth-spreading, 'But now me behooveth to see a little more of this forth-spreading.'

Foul-head, *foulness.*

Frackles, *freckles.*

Fragility, *frailty, weakness.*

Frey, *or* fray, *fright.*

Friendful, *friendly.*

Friendfully, *with fulness of friendship.*

Fro, *from.*

Fulfill, *to fill full, complete.*

Full-head, *or* Fulhed, *fulness, excellency.*

Fulsome, *plentiful.*

Fulsomeness, *perfect fulness, plenteousness.*

Fulsomelie, *plenteously, fully.*

G.

Game, *ridicule, sport, victory.*

Getten, *begotten?* 'For we are ordained thereto in kind, and getten thereto by grace.'

Getting, *taking, begetting.* 'And so getting his lively members.'

Giveth? 'And he ruleth and giveth heaven and earth and all that is.' 'The God-head ruleth and giveth.' 'He dwelleth here in us, and ruleth us, and giveth us in this living, and bringeth us to his bliss.'

God-head, *good-head, goodness.*

Goodhead, *goodness.*

Gramercy, *grant mercy.*

Greatelie, *greatly.*

Grievouser, *more grievous.*

Groneth, *groaneth.*

Grudge, *feel compunction? be reluctant.*

H.

Halse, *or* Haulse, *to embrace round the neck.*

Happ, *chance.*

Hard, *steadfast, keen, laborious, cruel, grievous.*

Hardy, *bold.*

Have, *to behave.*

Head, *or* Hood, *state or condition of any thing.*

Head-pann, *skull.*

Her? 'And for the roundness, they were like to the seal of her ring in the spreading of the forehead.'

Here, *before, before this.*

Herefore, *on this account?*

Heyward? 'And within him an heyward long and broad all full of endless heavenliness.' *I suppose an article of dress.* 'Going woolward,' *was wearing a coarse woollen garment for penance.*

Highed, *increased.*
Hill, *to conceal.*
Hold, *obliged.*
Holsomely, *wholesomely.*
Holy *or* Holly, *wholly, entirely.*
Holpen, *helped.*
Homelie, *familiar, friendly, intimate, domestic, plain, simple.*
Homelie, *truly, familiarly, intimately.*
Homliest, *most homely.*
Homly-head, *homeliness.*
Homlliness, *familiarity, intimacy, plainness.*
Honestlie, *seemly, comely.*
Horribility, *horrible nature.*
Horriblier, *more horrible.*

I.

Impropred, *appropriated.*
In, *upon.*
Indifferent, *ordinary?*
Intend, *to attend.*
Into, *unto.*
Into, *in two.* 'That the love of him and of our souls shall never be departed into without end.'
Irkeness, *irksomeness.*

K.

Kild, *killed.*
Kind, *nature, humanity.*
Kind, *or* Kindlie, *natural, loving.*
Kindly, *naturally.*
Kindle, *incite, stimulate, sharpen.* 'He kindleth our understanding.'
Kindness, *naturalness, nature?*
Kirtle, *a tunic or waistcoat.*
Knowing, *known.*

L.

Lack, *impediment, fault, disgrace, want.*
Langure, *to languish.*
Lean-head, *leanness.*
Leaver *or* levir, *rather, more willingly.*
Leese, *lose.*
Leesing, *losing.*
Lengeth, *lengtheneth.*
Lessed, *lessened.*
Let *or* Letting, *hindrance.*
Let, *to prevent, hinder.*
Lightlier, *lighter.*
Lightning, *enlightening, lighting.*
Like, *to please, to take pleasure in.*
Liken, *to like, to please.*
Likeness, *pleasure, delight.*
Likeness, *comparison.*
Liking, *appearance, likeness?*
Liking, *pleasure.*
Liking, *pleasureable.*
Litle, (v.) *lead.* 'One time my understanding was litle down into the sea-ground.'
Litle, *little.*
Litle-head, *littleness.*
Lively-head, *liveliness.*
Loath, *unwilling.*

Loathness, *unwillingness.*
Long, *to belong.*
Long, *to desire.*
Lore, *knowledge, doctrine, advice.*
Lother, *more unwilling.*
Lovesome, *lovely.*
Lowed, *humbled.*

M.

Manhead, *manhood, humanity.*
Manner, *kind or sort.* 'All manner vertues:' *all kind of vertues.*
Marvail, *or* Marveile, *wonder.*
Marvel, *to wonder.*
May, *to be able:* (used in the inf. m.) 'But our precious mother Jesu may feed us with himself:' *Is able to feed us with himself.*
Maym, *injury.*
Mean, *intervening, intermediate.*
Meane, *medium, instrument.* 'Without any mean:' *immediately.*
Meddled, *or* Medled, *mingled, two-fold.*
Medelur, *or* Medle, *mixture.*
Meed, *reward.*
Meedfully, *meritoriously.*
Meek, *to make meek or humble.*
Meek-head, *meekness.*
Mickle, *or* Mykill, *much.*
Middes, *midst, middle.*
Mid-face, *middle of the face, profile.*
Mid-head, *centre.*
Mid-point, *central point.*
Mids, *midst.*
Might, *power, strength.*
Mightest, *most mighty.*
Mightifully, *with fullness of might.*
Mightilier, *more mighty.*
Mightly, *mightily.*
Mind, *feeling, consideration, remembrance.*
Mischief, *misfortune.*
Mis-liking, *disliking.*
Misrule, *to disorder.*
Mistely, *darkly.*
Moneth, *moaneth.*
Morrow, *morning.*
Most, *perhaps for* 'moisture.' 'And also his most cloggering together and dried to my sight.' Chap. xvi.
Mote, *must, may.*
Mother-head, *or* Mother-hood, *state or condition of a mother, all which appertains to a mother.*
Mourningly, *mournfully.*

N.

Naught, *to empty, mock, bring to nothing.*
Naughting, *emptying, excepting?*
Naughting, *nothingness, worthlessness, short comings?* 'Our breakings and our naughtings.'
Near-hood, *nearness.*
Ne, (conj.) *nor.*

Ne, (adv.) not.
Nobility, *dignity, splendour.*
Noble, *perhaps for* 'nobley.' 'Which I saw him highly enjoy for the worshipful resting, and noble that he will, and shall bring his servant to by his plenteous grace.'
Noblety, *or* Nobletie, *nobleness: same as* Nobility.
Nobley, *or* Nobly, *dignity, splendour.*
Nobliest, *or* Noblest, *most noble.*
None, *probably for* Anon. *Purpose, design?* 'And none after this our blessed Lord gave me again of the comfort and the rest in soul.'
Noieth, *annoyeth.*
Not, *naught.*
Not but, *only.*
Nought *or* Naught, *nothing.*

O.

Of, *in.*
On, *in.*
One, *to unite.*
One-head, *oneness.*
Oned, Onid, *or* Onyd, *united.*
Ones, *once.* 'All at ones:' *all at once.*
Oning, *union.*
Oning, *uniting.*
Or, *before.* 'Or that:' *before that.*
Otherwhile, *at other times.*
Ought, *any thing.*
Out-passing, *expiring.*
Over, *far above.*
Over-laid, *over-borne.*
Over-more, *moreover.*
Over-parte, *upper part.*
Over-pass, *to excell, surpass.*
Over-passing, *excellence.*
Over-passing, *exceedingly.*
Over-yede, *overspread, covered.*
Owe, *ought.*
Own, *to unite.*
Owned, *united.*

P.

Paid, *satisfied, contented.*
Painfuller, *more painful.*
Parliament, *consultation, debate.*
Party, *part.*
Pass, *to die.*
Pass, *to surpass, excel.*
Passible, *capable of suffering.*
Passing, *transient.*
Passingly, *exceedingly.*
Paynius, *pagan.*
Peace, *to set at peace.*
Pearcing, *piercing.*
Pellets, *balls.*
Penance, *repentance.*
Perished, *lost, destroyed.* 'None shall be perished.'
Plainlie, *simply, clearly.*
Pleasaunce, *pleasantness, pleasure, delight.*
Pleasable, *pleasurable, agreeable?*
Plenteous-head, *plenteousness.*

Point in a, *with exactness, with precision, to a nicety?* 'I saw God in a point.' 'That we set the point of our thought:' *that we concentrate our thought?*

Praid, *entreated.*

Prayer, *pray?* 'For all the cause wherefore we prayer.'

Prime, *morning. It meant originally the first canonical hour of prayer.* 'Prime day:' *morning.*

Privities, *secrets, private affairs.*

Pronity, *grovelling.*

Protraid, *pourtrayed.*

Q.

Quick, *to make alive.*

R.

Raced, *or* Raised, *rased, scraped.*

Raigning, *reigning.*

Raising, *scraping.*

Ready, *prompt, on the alert.*

Redily, *readily.*

Reform, *to make anew.*

Religious person a, *one of a religious order, a clergyman.*

Resentment, *regard.*

Reserving? 'Reserving the worshipful thanks of God.'

Retchlesness, i. e. Wretchlessness, *or* Recklessness, *carelessness.*

Retchlesser, *more reckless, or careless.*

Retchesly, *recklessly, carelessly.*

Reproved, *reprobated?*

Reward, *to award, regard, respect?*

Rewly-head, i. e. Ruely-head, *ruefulness, grievousness, sorrowfulness.*

Rialty, *royalty.*

Richless, *reckless, careless.*

Right, *truly, exactly, completely.* 'Right as:' *just as.*

Rights, *offices, sacraments.*

Right full-head, *plenitude.*

Rightful-head, *rightfulness.*

Rightwise, *truly wise.*

Rimpild, *wrinkled.*

Roode-tree, *cross.*

Round-head, *roundness.*

Ruful, *or* Rufull, *rueful, pitiful, grievous.*

Ruth, *or* Rewthe, *pity, sorrow.*

S.

Sad, *firm, grave.*

Sadly, *firmly, gravely.*

Sadness, *firmness, consistency, gravity.*

Safe, *saved.*

Sagging, *drooping, hanging heavily like a wet cloth.*

Salve. 'And he is salve of our life.'

Same, *end?* 'But his wisdom and his love suffer not the same to come till the best time.'

Save, *to make good.*

See, *seat.*

Seelie, *simple, weak.*

Self, *same.*

Sennet, Sevenight; *the space of seven nights and days, a week.*
Setled, *settled.*
Shape, *form, figure.*
Shapely, *fit, proper.*
Sharply, *swiftly.*
Shrewdness, *wickedness, ill-nature.*
Shriven, *confessed and absolved.*
Shrowd, *wicked, malicious.*
Sicker, *or* Siker, *sure.*
Sickerness, *or* Sikerness, *security, assurance.*
Sickerly, surely.
Sickness, *sickerness?* 'For sickness and comfort against all tribulations that may come.'
Side, *long, ample, broad, spacious.* 'Wide and Side:' *wide and long.*
Sikerest, *most sure.*
Simple-head, *simpleness.*
Single-head, *singleness.*
Sithen, *or* Sithens, *since, afterwards.*
Slade, *valley, precipice.*
Slouth, *sloth.*
Sodaine, *sudden.*
Sodenlie, *or* Soudeinlie, *suddenly.*
Soft, *timorous, low, gentle, quiet.*
Somedeal, *somewhat, in some measure.*
Sooth, *truth.*
Soothly, *truly.*
Soothfastness, *truth.*
Soothnesse, *same as* Soothfastness.
Sothfastlie, *assuredly.*
Speed, *profit.*
Speed, *to profit, to despatch.*
Speedful, *profitable, useful, effectual.*
Standing, *understanding.*
Standing, *consistent with, in agreement with, becoming?*
Steed, *or* Stead, *resting-place.*
Streit, *straight, close.*
Stint, *to cease, stop.*
Stinted, *ceased, stopped.*
Stinting, *ceasing, stopping, limit.*
Stonnyed, *astonished, or stunned.*
Strengthed, *strengthened.*
Substanciallie, *with reality of existence, truly, really.*
Subtile, *exquisitely spun, exquisitely fine?*
Suffer, *to allow.*
Suffer, *to chasten?*
Sulloing, *sullying.*
Surety, *sureness, reality.*
Sweinly, *darkly, obscurely.*
Swemful, *obscure.*
Swilge, *foul, foulness.*

T.

Take, *taken.*
Than, *then.*
That, 'And all that fair vertues.'
That, (conj.) *because.*
That, pron. dem. used as a relative. *As much as. It is sometimes put for the same.*

The, 'And be diseased in divers manners for the own profit.' 'As it seemeth to the self.'
Themself, *themselves.*
Then, *than.*
There, *frequently used in the sense of,* Where.
Therefro, *therefrom.*
Theron, *thereon.*
Therto, *thereto.* Ther *in composition signifies* 'that,' *without including any idea of place.*
Tho, *those.*
Threateth, *threateneth.*
To, *in composition with verbs is generally augmentative.*
Token, *mark, plague-spot.*
To fore, *or* To for, *before.*
Travaile, *or* Travel, *toil, labour, fatigue.*
Travel, *to labour, to toil, to be in anguish, to give pain.*
Travellous, *grievous, distressing.*
Treat, *negotiate, carry on, settle.*
Trowe, *to think, trust.*

U.

Unableness, *feebleness, inability.*
Unbegun, *without beginning.*
Unchristen, *unchristian.*
Uncunning, *want of cunning, or skill.*
Undeparted, *undivided.*
Under-sett, *propped up.*
Understand, *understood.*
Undertake, *to receive.*
Undiscreetly, *indiscreetly.*
Un-fore-sight, *want of foresight.*
Unied? *united.*
Uning, *union.*
Unkind, *unnatural.*
Unknowing, *ignorance.*
Unlettered, *unlearned.*
Unloathful, *unspotted.*
Unlothful, *willing.*
Unlothfulness, *willingness.*
Unmight, *weakness, impotency.*
Unmighty, *weak.*
Unneath, Unnethes, Unneth, *or* Uneth, *scarcely.*
Unpassible, *incapable of suffering.*
Unpatience, *impatience.*
Unpeace, *disquietude.*
Unpossible, *impossible.*
Unrest, *want of rest, uneasiness, trouble.*
Unsickerness, *insecurity, frailty.*
Unskillful, *unreasonable, injurious.*
Unwise, *foolish.*
Unwitting, *not knowing.*
Up, *according to.* 'And eschew venial (sins) reasonably up our might.'
Up-risen, *raised again, in a resurrection state.*
Up-rising, *resurrection.*
Utter, *outward.*

V.

Venial, *pardonable.* Venial sin: *in contradistinction to mortal sin.*

Vernacle, *diminutive of* Veronike, *a copy in miniature of the picture of Christ which is fabled to have been miraculously imprinted on a handkerchief, preserved in the Church of St. Peter at Rome.*

Verie, *or* Very, *real, true.*

Verily, *really, truly.*

Vertue, *power, strength, efficacy.*

Vertuous, *powerful, efficacious.*

W.

Wallow, *roll about.*

Ware, *aware.* 'But be we ware.'

Wax, *grow.*

Weal, *wealth, prosperity, happiness.*

Ween, *or* Wene, *to suppose, think.*

Went, *or* Wende, *thought.*

Which, *what.*

Whiles, the, *meanwhile.*

Whistering, *whispering.*

Whole-head, *wholeness, fullness.*

Wide. 'Side and Wide:' *far and widely.*

Wilfull, *earnest.*

Wilfullie, *earnestly, seriously, willingly.*

Willingfully, *willingly.*

Wise, *manner.*

Wist, *knew.* 'For that would I a wist dreadful:' *I desired with fear to have known. I longed exceedingly to have known.*

Wistly, *wistfully, earnestly, with eager attention.*

Wit, *to know.*

Wit, *knowledge.*

Witsafe, *vouchsafed.*

Wonning, *dwelling.*

Worfully, *worthfully? honorably? worshipfully? full worthily?* 'And then he should take the meat with the drink, and bear it full worfully before the Lord.'

Worken, *work, or worked.*

Worthy, *in a state fitted for any thing.* 'Which may never be known into the time that God of his goodness hath made us worthy to see it. *There is a provincial usage of the word* 'worthy' *still in existence.* 'We were not worthy to know it.' 'If I had been worthy to know that you were there I would have met you.'

Worshipfullest, *most worshipful.*

Wot, *or* Wote, *knew.*

Wrake, *sea-weed?*

Wretchedful, *full of wretchedness.*

Wrieth, *writheth.*

Y.

Ye, *old form of*, Yea. 'Ye so far forth I saw that our Lord enjoyeth of the tribulation of his servants.'

Yield, *to give, or yield a reward; applied to God, to bless.* 'And in our good Lord the Holy Ghost we have our rewarding, and our yielding for our living and our travel. So,

"Tend me to-night two hours, I ask no more,
And the Gods yield you for it."
ANT. AND CLEOP. iv. 2.